FORBIDDEN STATISTICS

Non-Western Immigrant Crime in Europe

Joseph R. Oxfield

DEDICATION

I dedicate this work to all the victims of crime. In Europe, and around the world. However, I want to dedicate it specifically to those that died on the continent of Europe at the hands of non-Western immigrants. For they died a needless death, enabled by 'progressive' governments that believe in open borders.

CONTENTS

ACKNOWLEDGMENTS

I wish to thank all those that have taken the time and effort to track news on migrant crime events and statistics. If a tree falls in a forest, and there was nobody there to hear it, did it make a sound? It is important that we report on these kinds of events, to let people know what happens. To bring the truth about.

"Who controls the past controls the future: who controls the present controls the past."

THE BIG QUESTION

"He reminds me of the man who murdered both his parents, and then when the sentence was about to be pronounced, pleaded for mercy on the grounds that he was orphan."
– Abraham Lincoln

We must ask what have the migrants brought to us. Are they peaceful and eager to integrate? Or do they violate the laws of the land? The news is plentiful, and it can be difficult to see the forest through the trees. The top results on Google for 'migrant crime in Europe' show an article by Reason [1] and an article by the BBC [2]. Both articles conclude that the scare of migrant crime is greatly exaggerated. The articles imply that migrants cause no more crime or misconduct than the native populations of the European lands. This goes against a gut feeling present in many Europeans. It goes against the commonly held belief that migrant areas are less safe. In addition, it begs the question; is it all just a misplaced racist concept? Do they really affect the safety of the area, or is it far-right propaganda?

This book sets out to investigate and discover the truth. Not limited to one country, but with a detailed overview of all European countries that have seen large inflows of migrants over the last decades. The United Kingdom, Ireland, Sweden, Finland, Norway, Germany, the Netherlands, Belgium, France, Italy, Austria, Spain, Greece, and Portugal. How has the arrival of migrants in these countries impacted crime and safety? Are there any changes? Is there any identifiable impact that we can ascribe to the arrival of migrants?

What I will not talk about as much is migrant on migrant crime that does not really bring problems for the native populations of Europe. This includes female genital mutilation, a practice brought over from Africa where a woman's, or better said, a girl's genitals are mutilated so that she will not experience sexual satisfaction, and thereby be more likely to remain a virgin. As horrible as such practices are, it is irrelevant for the average German person if this happens to their neighbor, or to a girl still living in Africa. In the end, it does not affect them personally in their daily life. Nobody is forcing them to apply female genital mutilation to their own German daughter. There is no increase in suffering in the European population. The same logic applies to honor killings and acid attacks, generally perpetrated by Muslims that are dissatisfied with the behavior of their own family. As horrible as these crimes are, and they truly are – nobody deserves a batch of acid thrown in their face for seeing a boy that their father does not approve of – this is not the topic I seek to research in this book.

I aim to combine the anecdotal evidence, in the form of news reports regarding individual cases, with hard statistical evidence based on government data. Unfortunately, such statistical evidence is often not available, as many countries prefer to hide this inconvenient truth. Concerning references, I have decided to include a reference number in the text, usually at the end of the paragraph. At the end of the chapter, you can find a link to the source webpage. This, I believe, is the easiest way for anyone to double-check that what I have written is true. There is always the risk that some articles were translated wrong, or even reported falsely in the original report. I do not expect this to be the case, but I do not want to exclude the possibility regarding some of the minor examples. It may be expected that for those reading this book a decade from today, many of these websites will be offline. Websites that tracked many migrant crimes, such as voiceofeurope.com or theoldcontinent.eu have already ceased to exist. Since advertisers shy away from the controversy surrounding the topic, it is impossible to turn a profit. Hence, the sharing of such information depends on willing volunteers, eager to invest time and money. It may also be expected that more governments have ceased tracking such statistics a decade from today, afraid of the backlash that comes in the form of electoral victories for right-wing parties. I would say it is not unlikely that the European Union decides to completely ban national governments from publishing such statistics, using some argument related to discrimination or equality.

This is regrettable, and I can only say that at least by holding a physical copy of this book, you ensure that these crimes are not forgotten. For the sake of their victims, so that they too may not be forgotten.

Before we get started, I wish to highlight once more that when talking statistics and averages, we do not talk about the individual. We talk about the group. That a group is on average more criminal does not mean that every individual in the group is a criminal, and I have no intention of claiming that to be the case. Nevertheless, if a group is indeed more criminal, it does impact the rest of the population as a whole. Again, not everyone will become a victim, but more people will. Not every dog with rabies will bite you, but statistically, they are more likely to do so, hence we stay away. Statistically, old Soviet airplanes are more likely to crash than the new Airbus. Not every plane will crash, but we tend to stay away. Statistically, you are more likely to get robbed when you don't lock your door. So we lock our doors to reduce the risk. Somehow, we don't want to lock our national borders for the same reason.

"The dead cannot cry out for justice. It is a duty of the living to do so for them."

- Lois McMaster Bujold

Notes

[1]   https://reason.com/2020/09/15/the-myth-of-europes-migrant-crisis/

[2]   https://www.bbc.com/news/world-europe-45419466

IRELAND, THE EMERALD ISLE

Requiescat

All her bright golden hair
Tarnished with rust,
She that was young and fair
Fallen to dust.

Lily-like, white as snow,
She hardly knew
She was a woman, so
Sweetly she grew ...

- Oscar Wilde

Migration is not a new phenomenon in Ireland. A country once ravaged by the potato famine has discovered the benefits of being a tax paradise for large multinational internet-firms. Google, Facebook, Amazon, and others have moved their offices into Dublin. This, in combination with Ireland joining the European Union, has not only opened their borders, but made it an attractive destination for migrants. Simultaneously, it is obviously not the easiest place to migrate to. Being an island located on the western edge of Europe, it takes a bit more effort to find your way towards it, than a country like Spain. This mixture explains why Ireland sees a relatively high degree of

Eastern Europeans that legally migrated to find work, while simultaneously seeing relatively few illegal immigrants from places like Africa.

Immigrant Gangs

Already in 2002, an article in the Irish Independent highlighted the changing face of Irish crime. 'Only a year or two ago, the profile of prisoners in the recreation yard of Cloverhill Prison was almost entirely Dublin working class. The home-grown inmate population has now been supplemented by dozens of foreigners including African drug smugglers and more than 30 young Chinese, along with other groups including Nigerians, Albanians, Kosovars, Romanians, and a few from other eastern European States. The number of foreign nationals in custody here has reached its highest levels.' [1]

Apparently, back in 2002, newspapers were still allowed to express serious concern about the uncontrolled inflow of immigrants. The article continues with, 'There are, however, concerns that the State's biggest influx of immigrants is being used as a cover for some of the organised crime groups which have been spreading west from the former Soviet states and arriving from China and west Africa.' Organized crime exists in many places in the world, and they are more than happy to abuse the low-control open-border system that Europe has descended into. 'The gardai [the national police of the Irish Republic] also report increasing activity by Chinese gangs. These are believed to involve newly-arrived members of Triad gangs.' Such gangs bring violence, fraud, and international drug trafficking to Ireland. 'Nigeria, a country beset by corruption, has produced fraudsters on an industrial scale and the 419 named after a section of the Nigerian Criminal Code dealing with fraud has become a problem on an international scale.'

'The 419 is responsible for the infamous "advance fees" fraud where victims receive an email or fax pretending that the sender has access to a huge amount of money stuck in an African bank that needs to be expatriated. The victim is then asked to lodge a sum of money in a joint account so the millions can then be moved out of Africa. The "advance fee" is then stolen. This scam has caught out hundreds of gullible victims.'

'Nigerians are now believed responsible for organizing huge welfare fraud here and in the UK, using false identities so that immigrants can claim benefits in either state. Gardai know this is taking place but have great difficulty proving cases. The 419 has developed into a very sophisticated, wide-ranging international criminal conspiracy with leading members now in charge of high-tech credit card fraud and, in recent years, drug smuggling. Some fifty Africans, many of them poor white South Africans who were used as cocaine- and cannabis-smuggling "mules", have been caught at Dublin Airport while carrying drugs for a Nigerian "Mr. Big".'

Not to ignore the presence of the Albanians, the article continues. 'The latest group of which gardai are now increasingly wary is suspected members of the Albanian and Kosovan mafias. Already regarded as the most violent new arrivals in the rest of Europe's organized crime scene, their presence here is just beginning to be felt, according to gardai. The Albanian gangsters are generally men in their 20s from the backward northern part of their country. It is believed they are organized into clans, bound by an ancient code of honor called Kanun. Throughout Europe, the Albanians have a reputation for extreme violence and involvement in prostitution.'

Additional problems arise for the Irish when they seek to deport illegal immigrants. Due to the open border system, these migrants can simply disappear. Either they are hiding somewhere within Ireland, or, just as likely, have crossed the border. 'No exit checks are carried out at Irish ports, airports or along the border with the North. That means it is impossible to determine if migrants who effectively go missing from the international protection, or asylum, system have left the State or remain here. According to figures from the Department of Justice, between 2011 and October 2018, some 9,197 deportation orders were made and 1,857 resulted in deportation.' [2]

Although the Nigerian gangs are not restricted to Ireland, the country forms a part of their area of control. 'Highly organised Nigerian gangs are earning "extremely high profits" from trafficking children into 12 European countries, including Ireland, for prostitution, according to the EU police agency. Europol said victims generate a smuggling debt of between €30,000-€60,000 each — and that paying off the debts can take years. The agency said Nigerian criminal groups are organised into cells, typically run by females, known as "madams", with men working in supportive roles. The Europol report on the trafficking and exploitation of underage victims said southern EU countries, such as Italy and Spain, are the main entry points for trafficked Nigerians. It said victims are then forced into prostitution in both the two entry countries and ten other member states, including Ireland. It said Nigerian organised crime gangs pose a "great challenge" to EU law enforcement. It said they were well organised, but not structured like most other crime networks.' [3] The age of the girls tends to sit between fifteen and seventeen, but younger girls are smuggled into Europe as well. Some cases include girls younger than five years old.

The presence of Albanian and Nigerian mafia has not declined over the years. An article from 2019 details a bust made on a group of Albanians, believed to be active in both people smuggling and drug trading. They remain active in Ireland. [4]

Conversion to Islam

Meanwhile, integration seems to take a reverse route in Ireland, as it is estimated that around five-hundred Irish convert to Islam every year. The converts are mostly women. The reason is mostly for marriage. [5] In 2018, the famous (at least in Ireland and parts of Europe) singer Sinead O'Connor even converted to Islam. [6]

Beyond these active gangs, Ireland does not appear too strongly influenced by migrant crime, and continues to be a mostly safe country. Going on holiday to Gran Canaria may be more dangerous than staying put in Ireland, as in early 2021 four illegal immigrants from Africa were convicted for gang raping an Irish woman that visited as a tourist. [7]

It is noteworthy that most of the migrants to Ireland were Europeans, notably from the Baltics, Balkans, and Poles. Muslims form only between one and two percent of the population so far. A tiny amount compared to places like the United Kingdom or France.

The Lake Isle of Innisfree

I will arise and go now, for always night and day
I hear lake water lapping with low sounds by the shore;
While I stand on the roadway, or on the pavements grey,
I hear it in the deep heart's core.

W.B. Yeats

Notes

[1] https://www.independent.ie/irish-news/organised-violent-crime-is-spiralling-among-the-non-national-population-26243687.html

[2] https://www.irishtimes.com/news/crime-and-law/migrants-can-simply-leave-ireland-or-disappear-1.4093757

[3] https://www.irishexaminer.com/news/arid-30897094.html

[4] https://www.irishtimes.com/news/crime-and-law/alleged-albanian-people-trafficker-raided-by-criminal-assets-bureau-1.4107027

[5] https://www.independent.ie/lifestyle/lifting-the-veil-on-irish-islam-29941427.html

[6] https://www.bbc.com/news/entertainment-arts-45987127

[7] https://www.euroweeklynews.com/2021/03/03/illegal-immigrants-to-appear-in-court-for-alleged-gang-rape/

SEXUAL VIOLENCE IN SWEDEN

"People in Sweden are very conscious of what people are saying about you."
- Avicii

Sweden has been one of the big destinations of the 2015 migrant wave flooding Europe. The Swedish government has been very welcoming towards the newcomers, and insists that a new Swedish identity will be formed between all different nations inhabiting their land.

What's happening in Sweden?

During the 2016, President Donald Trump put the spotlight on Sweden when he said 'You look at what's happening in Germany, you look at what's happening last night in Sweden. Sweden, who would believe this. Sweden. They took in large numbers. They're having problems like they never thought possible.'

Well, his comment was highly scrutinized afterwards, but let us have a look at what has happened in Sweden.

Statistics

We can be clear and scientific about the fact that immigrants are highly overrepresented in the Swedish crime statistics. First and second generation immigrants form 33% of the population in Sweden, but they form 58% of crime suspects. That percentage rises to 72% when it is narrowed to the crimes of murder and manslaughter. For robbery, the percentage is 70%. For rape and attempted rape, the percentage is just below 60%. If migrants would be just as criminal as the native Swedes, all percentages should be that same 33%.

A theoretical removal of all immigrants and their descendants from Sweden would immediately reduce murder, manslaughter, and robbery, by more than 70%. [2] Unfortunately in Sweden the data is not split between Western and non-Western immigrants, so we are missing a bit of granular detail. Migrants from Finland and Norway, or Denmark and Germany, are likely not the ones driving up crime rates. I say likely, but the data from Sweden does not prove that of course. Data in other countries may. Anecdotal evidence from Sweden may already point us in a certain direction.

Gang Violence

Sweden's gang violence consists of Muslim groups armed with AK-47's and hand grenades. The Spectator had a 2019 article titled 'Bomb attacks are now a normal part of Swedish life. Gang violence is now at a level where it threatens to undermine the Swedish state.' [3] The article starts with the following description of a night in the Swedish capital of Stockholm, 'One night last week, explosions took place in three different locations in and around Stockholm. There were no injuries this time, just the usual shattered windows, scattered debris and shocked people woken by the blast. The police bomb squad was already on its way to the first explosion in the district of Vaxholm when it had to turn around and prioritize the detonation at a residential building in the more densely populated city center. Residents whose doors had been deformed by the shock wave had to be rescued. The third target (seemingly unrelated) was a facility belonging to a Syrian Orthodox church, which had already been bombed twice in the past year.'

Wilhelm Agrell, professor of intelligence analysis at Lund University, considers it a jeopardy to the integrity of the Swedish state. 'The state's monopoly on violence, the actual token of a sovereign government, has been hollowed out bit by bit and no longer exists. The armed criminal violence is having effects that are increasingly similar to those of terrorism.'

When a government cannot control the violence in the country, we would refer to it as a failed state. That is why we call Libya a failed state. Perhaps Sweden manages to escape this prerogative by being located in Europe. Or perhaps it is because most parts of Sweden are still safe and under control. Due to immigration, Sweden has risen from being at the bottom of crime-rankings in Europe, to being at the top. A dubious honor.

Sweden is also notorious for being the rape capital of Europe. Although not being responsible for more than 60% of all rapes, immigrants are responsible for 80% of 'stranger rape'. Stranger rape refers to the victim and perpetrator not knowing one another, and fits to the stereotypical rape where a girl is pulled into the bushes by a stranger. Half of the immigrant stranger rapes were committed by men that had been in Sweden for less than a year. [4] The perpetrators mostly originated from Africa and the Middle East, with Afghanistan taking the top spot. To reiterate, there are hordes of men supposedly fleeing the war in Afghanistan, only to arrive in Sweden and begin raping Swedish women. Do such people deserve to be saved from a warzone? Can stranger rape be blamed on socio-economic factors? This overrepresentation in stranger rape is something that will repeat in every country we look at.

The gangs do not stop their activities at explosions, which frequently take place in residential areas. Fatal shootings occur frequently, dozens every year in a country with only ten million inhabitants. Their comparable neighbor Norway, which has far fewer migrants, has only a fraction of such events taking place. Fitting to the story, nine out of ten perpetrators in gang shootings are immigrants or their children. The victims, on the other hand, are not always gangsters themselves. The story in the Spectator mentions an example of a young woman being executed in cold blood, 'a young woman was murdered in an affluent neighbourhood in Malmö, in an attack which police believe was aimed at her boyfriend. Karolin... was carrying her young child when she was gunned down. As she was lying on the ground, the shooter put a bullet in her head. Her baby is now in a government protection programme.'

Not only are the partners of men active in the gang world targeted, innocent bystanders are not infrequently hurt by collateral damage. In the summer of 2020 a twelve-year-old girl was hit by a stray bullet while walking her dog, she died on the spot. These are the kinds of incidents that make people live in fear. [6]

A Swedish police commander decided to speak out on the topic of migrant crime. Mats Löfving, the deputy national police chief, opened the book on 40-plus family-based criminal networks, or clans, operating in the country. 'They are made up of immigrants who came to Sweden solely for the purpose of organising and systematising crime, making their money through drug-trafficking and extortion. and possessing a great capacity for violence.' [5] The Swedish government refuses to acknowledge any connection between migrants and the increase in crime in Sweden over the last years.

Terror in Stockholm

It is also worth noting who the perpetrator was in the 2017 terrorist attack where a man drove a truck into a department store in the center of Stockholm. The perpetrator was an Uzbeki Muslim whose request for asylum had been denied. Police hadn't been able to deport him, since they hadn't been able to find him. His name was Rakhmat Akilov. [7] Four people died in this attack. Lena Wahlberg, 69, from Sweden, Chris Bevington, 41, from Britain and Maïlys Dereymaeker, 31, from Belgium. Lastly, there was the eleven-year-old Ebba Akerlund, from Sweden. She was a young girl walking home from school. [8]

Full Denial

The Swedish government refuses to conduct further studies into the connections between crime and migration background. 'It does not matter to me if you are black or white, once you commit a crime you should be punished, that's my starting point.' according to the Swedish Minister of Justice Morgan Johansson. [9] Nobody denies that those that commit a crime should be punished; they just wish to analyze the data and look for a correlation in demographics and crime. The anti-science stance from the Swedish government, which appears afraid that the scientific results would play into the hands of the far-right, actually acknowledges that the far-right has a point when it comes to migrants and crime. Science is only useful when it serves your own agenda, or so it seems.

The Cemetery

The government can pretend nothing strange is going on, but frequent news reports tend to disagree. In the summer of 2020, two underage boys were found naked, stabbed, beaten, and raped, half-buried alive in a cemetery in Sweden. The two young boys were Swedish, the two perpetrators were Iranian and Tunisian. They had kidnapped the boys, beaten them, stabbed them, told them to remove all their clothes, raped them, and buried them in the cemetery. A gruesome crime. The event appears to have been triggered by the two Swedish boys refusing to buy drugs from the perpetrators. The boys were found the next morning, after having spent the night naked and buried in the cemetery. It is unclear as to how deeply they were buried, but apparently somewhere in between having enough room to breathe, yet being unable to move. The Iranian was twenty one-years-old and had arrived in Sweden in 2009 as a child refugee. The eighteen-year-old Tunisian was born in Sweden to immigrant parents. Both were known to the police, for burglary and throwing Molotov cocktails. [10]

Don't want to get raped? Stay home.

How does the police react to violent crimes? Well, one time it warned women to stay home or only go out in pairs, after three violent gang rapes took place in Malmo in under a month. That was in 2017. Such advice is an admission of defeat, an admission that you cannot protect your own citizens walking around alone. [11]

One of the rapes involved a seventeen-year-old girl, raped by a group of strangers on a playground.

Another woman was raped on her way home from a party, while the third was standing at a bus stop before being attacked by a group of men and raped. The events sparked outrage and protests, but a relatively small crowd of hundreds of people were the only ones to participate in these protests. Some, it seems, were more outraged by the statements made by their government, warning them to stay home, than about the perpetrators. In all cases, the perpetrators were immigrant men.

Malmo, located in the south of Sweden, used to be a nice, quiet town, though today it is a hotspot of violence and rape. Coincidentally, it is also one of the locations with the most immigrants. Most of them live in the flats in the suburbs, while the city center remains okay.

A year earlier, in 2016, a gang rape in Gotland on a wheelchair-bound woman by asylum seekers led to protesters attacking the asylum center. [12] This woman was already in a wheelchair, but a previous gang rape from 2011 targeting a different woman was so severe that an otherwise healthy woman ended up in a wheelchair. [13]

The woman was lured to an asylum center where she was violently raped by eight, possibly nine, Afghan men. She now resides in a psychiatric institution, as she suffers from severe panic attacks. The article mentions she suffers fecal incontinence - you may understand the necessary damage dealt to reach such an outcome.

What did the accused have to say for themselves? They defended their action by saying the woman was 'bad', and 'a whore'. One of the perpetrators had raped four other women before, though somehow was still not jailed, and was not eligible for deportation because he had arrived in Sweden as a child refugee.

In 2017, the world was shocked by a rape in Sweden once more. This time, a three-hour livestream on Facebook showed the gang rape of a girl in Sweden. [14] It is definitely not very smart to broadcast your crimes on Facebook, but luckily, they did. Someone browsing through their timeline saw the livestream, and alerted the police. You might wonder what kind of a person would not only rape a woman, but rape her with a gang, and on top of that decide to livestream the event on Facebook. It shows a remorseless person that enjoys the deed and the humiliation that the victim suffers.

As horrible as it is for the regular Swedish woman, the outcome is even worse for the Swedish underclass. A female junkie went into a 'no-go zone' to buy drugs, and was instead attacked and raped by a group of twenty men. She was left for dead, while witnesses and people passing by refused to help her. A passerby commented that she had sperm on her face and clothes and he did not want to get involved. That wasn't the most horrible part of the story, however. The men were all judged to be not guilty, because they stated the woman agreed to the gang rape in exchange for drugs. That result came despite the woman having injuries on her body, and making her way to the hospital after the assault. She had been kicked, beaten, and threatened with a knife. Does that sound like a consensual exchange? That selling drugs, as well as prostitution, is illegal, was apparently ignored during the case. [15] News on the acquittal led to outrage and protests. [16]

There appears to be a trend where the perpetrators do not feel guilty for their crimes, but instead lack all respect or compassion for the victims. In another instance, a Swedish boy was humiliated, laughed at, and urinated on, by a group of migrants. [17] This goes far beyond simple bullying, and would be considered a hate crime if it was Swedish boys acting this way towards an immigrant child. Somehow, hate crimes appear to only work one way. Odd, considering the fact that migrants seem to target specifically the native Swedish population. Crimes appear motivated by a lack of respect towards the victims. This is a theme we will see occur over and over again in various countries.

Refugees Welcome

Despite the crime, the Swedes remain welcoming. In an instance where an Afghan man was on a plane bound for deportation, a Swedish girl bought a plane ticket on the same plane, in an attempt to prevent his deportation. She livestreamed her protest, she refused to sit down until the man was taken off the plane, on Facebook. [18] The man's request for asylum was rejected, but the misguided girl believed her actions would save his life as he was likely to get killed in Afghanistan.

It is clear that the girl has no idea what the situation in Afghanistan is like, believing everyone is likely to get killed immediately after setting foot on Afghan soil. Afghanistan may not be safe, but it is safer than she believes it to be. Such misconceptions may play a large role in Swedish attitudes towards refugees, as they have a severe overestimation of how dangerous the situation in these warzones is. Meanwhile, they underestimate the dangers presented by groups of migrants in their own country.

"The fastest way to destroy a culture is to make it multicultural."

— Robert Black

Notes:

[1]   https://www.bbc.com/news/world-us-canada-39020962

[2] https://link.springer.com/article/10.1007/s12115-019-00436-8

[3]   https://www.spectator.co.uk/article/bomb-attacks-are-now-a-normal-part-of-swedish-life

[4]   https://www.dailymail.co.uk/news/article-6095121/Eight-10-stranger-rapes-Sweden-carried-migrants-study-reveals.html

[5]   https://www.spectator.co.uk/article/swedens-crime-problem-has-become-too-big-to-ignore

[6]   https://www.bbc.com/news/world-europe-53581473

[7]   https://www.bbc.com/news/world-europe-39552691

[8]   https://www.dailymail.co.uk/news/article-4403032/Girl-11-killed-Stockholm-terror-attack-named.html

[9] https://sputniknews.com/europe/201802071061428402-sweden-norway-migrants-crime/

[10]   https://www.news.com.au/world/europe/two-teen-boys-tortured-raped-and-buried-alive-in-sweden/news-story/a951159e2fc7396a27a3d01ad3a268e6

[11]   https://www.dailymail.co.uk/news/article-5197675/Hundreds-protest-Sweden-series-gang-rapes.html

[12] https://www.independent.co.uk/news/world/europe/sweden-refugee-centre-attacked-rape-disabled-woman-gotland-claims-a7355186.html

[13]   http://www.pmclauth.com/news/worst-gang-rape-in-the-history-of-sweden

[14] https://www.news.com.au/technology/online/social/swedish-woman-gangraped-for-three-hours-live-on-facebook/news-story/fe7cf9c674fe9df21464f052b00c7f62

[15]   https://www.thelocal.se/20171219/five-men-acquitted-in-fittja-rape-case

[16]   https://www.sbs.com.au/news/an-embarrassment-anger-in-sweden-over-gang-rape-acquittals

[17]   https://summit.news/2019/12/17/sweden-migrant-gang-beat-urinate-on-teenager/

[18]   https://www.bbc.com/news/world-europe-44948604

FUCKING FINLAND

"Emergency does not read the law."
– Finnish saying

Being located in the far northeast of Europe, the cold and dark Finland is not the first place an immigrant would want to go. Still, their expansive welfare state and willingness to do their part in taking in immigrants entering the European Union has turned Finland multicultural. When I visited Helsinki a decade ago, you could already see the capital changing. Here too, we can see an impact on crime.

Rapes

In 2014 more than a thousand rapes were reported to the police in Finland. When you compare the suspects, it turns out that immigrants, relative to the total population, are three times more likely to be suspect of having committed a rape. [1] The victims, on the other hand, are more likely to be native Finns.

Research done into the topic shows the same conclusion. Immigrants are more likely to engage in criminal behavior. 'Our results show that, among immigrants, many forms of delinquency were more prevalent than among native youth. In particular, violent behavior and drug use appear to be more common for immigrants. In addition, immigrant youth who commit crimes reported more repeated offences than natives.' [2] Proponents of immigration will then aim to explain such differences in such a way that renders them irrelevant. However, the researchers accounted for this and found that the difference persists, even when taking into account multiple other possible influences. 'We controlled for family structure and the perceived relative affluence of the family, parental social control, and routine activities, such as staying out late at night and drinking alcohol. We also took into account morality, level of self-control and the academic achievement (GPA) of the respondents. Controlling for these factors decreased the immigrants' higher risk of active delinquency compared with native adolescents, but the difference remained significant.'

Finland was shaken by the news of a ten-year-old Finnish girl getting raped by a group of immigrant men. The girl had been contacted online, and seems to have agreed to meet one of the men out in the real world. Instead of a friendly meet-up, the man and his friends raped her. It is not clear from the story if the man pretended to be a child himself, or if they offered her gifts - both common tactics used in such 'grooming' practices. [3]

The event took place in Oulu, a relatively small town in Finland with just over 200.000 inhabitants. Such grooming took place consistently over years in the town, perpetrated by immigrant men. In 2018 several men were sentenced to around four years in jail each, for the grooming and raping of a then twelve-year-old girl. Outrage broke out once more at the ridiculously low penalties. [4]

All the victims were underage Finnish girls, while all perpetrators were foreign-born men. One of the victims ended up committing suicide as a direct result of the rape.

Not only young girls are desired. A woman born in the year 1930 was assaulted and raped in a laundry room in the same town. [5] Edward Dutton, a professor at the University of Oula (his exact role and connection to the university appears to be disputed), has written an entire book specifically regarding the Oula rape epidemic. It is titled 'The Silent Rape Epidemic; How Finns Were Groomed To Love Their Abusers'. [6] In this book I will stick to the previously discussed highlights, rather than expanding it as Dutton has done. For those interested, his book is available on Amazon.

Such crimes are, as one may expect, not restricted to Oulu. Helsinki too saw a brutal gang rape in 2015. Multiple Somalian men, born in Finland to Somalian parents, followed, attacked, and raped a Finnish girl. The Gatestone Institute reports 'The Tapanila rape shocked the quiet suburb, which lies on the outskirts of Helsinki, and all of Finland too. Many were left wondering why these second-generation Somali citizens of Finland would carry out such a savage attack.' [7] The Gatestone Institute continues, 'On the evening of November 23, 2015, a 14-year-old girl was walking home in Kempele, when a 17-year-old immigrant from Afghanistan attacked and raped her.

She was later found by locals walking through the area. A police dog led authorities to a nearby refugee center for underage asylum seekers.'

We may consider hospitality a great virtue, but it is also a common belief that guests should be kind to their hosts. Most proponents of open borders would vehemently defend the right of a seventeen-year-old Afghan to enter the country. After all, he is not only a child, but he is also coming from a warzone. Both valid points, but even a person like this, as the evidence shows, can abuse their welcome and decide to rape an innocent Finnish girl – someone's daughter. When Europe's hospitality is abused repeatedly, at what point is it justified to change our policies?

"A name doesn't make a man worse if the man doesn't make the name worse."

– Finnish saying

Notes:

[1] http://www.stat.fi/til/polrik/2014/04/polrik_2014_04_2015-01-19_fi.pdf

[2] https://journals.sagepub.com/doi/10.1177/1477370815587768

[3] https://www.thesun.co.uk/news/7917239/migrant-grooming-gang-oulu-finland/

[4] https://www.jihadwatch.org/2020/04/finland-muslim-rape-gang-that-repeatedly-sexually-assaulted-12-year-old-girl-gets-short-sentences

[5] https://finlandtoday.fi/man-22-jailed-for-suspected-rape-of-an-elderly-woman-in-the-laundry-room-in-oulu/

[6] https://www.amazon.de/-/en/Edward-Dutton/dp/1799003647

[7] https://www.gatestoneinstitute.org/7559/finland-migrant-crisis

FATALITY IN FRANCE

"There is a painful joke that Europeans often tell of their Gallic neighbors: God created France, the most beautiful country in the world with so much good in it, and ended up feeling guilty about it. He had to do something to make it fair. And so, he created the French people."

- Janine di Giovanni

France, perhaps the first real nation-state in Europe. Once the proud defender of European soil from its invaders, as it ended the rise of the caliphate at the battle of Toulouse in 721. Duke Odo of Aquitaine defeated the Islamic invaders that had already conquered the Iberian Peninsula. Without it, Europe could have turned Islamic over a thousand years ago. There were no great Christian powers to defend the rest of the continent. It was here in France that Charlemagne brought back stability to Europe and ended the dark ages.

Terrorism

Islamic terror in France began with Mohammed Merah. A jihadist that shot and killed seven people over a period of several days. One was a rabbi, three of them were schoolchildren. [22]

In 2013, another jihadist attacked a French policeman with a knife at 'La Defense'. [23] One year

34

later, 2014, a stabbing at the Tours police station by a man shouting 'Allahu Akbar'. [24] Three officers were wounded, the jihadist was killed.

In 2015, simultaneous with the migrant crisis, we see the first major attack. [16] The office of Charlie Hebdo, a satirical magazine, is attacked by jihadists, the Kouachi brothers, over a cartoon picture of their prophet. They are assisted by a third jihadist attacking a kosher supermarket. They kill seventeen people.

Later that same year a Jewish community center was attacked, three guards were wounded. [25] In the same year an Algerian in Villejuf wants to attack two churches, kills a woman while trying to steal her car, and prevents his plan from happening by accidentally shooting himself in the leg (Divine intervention? Immediate retribution? Karma?). [26]

June 2015 sees the first beheading, when Yassin Salhi executes his employer. [20] He then tries to blow up a building, but fails. Two months later a man tries to commit mass murder on the Thalys (a fast train) from Paris to Amsterdam, though other passengers manage to overpower him. His name was Ayoub el Khazzani. [21] He had wanted to take revenge for the bombings on Syria.

November 2015, the greatest terrorist attack of all. The infamous Bataclan bloodbath. Jihadists attacked the crowd at an Eagles of Death Metal concert. They succeeded in killing 131 people, injuring hundreds more. It was the deadliest attack on France since the Second World War. Besides Bataclan, the terrorists attacked crowded restaurants, and led an attack on a football stadium. [19]

The first of January 2016, a jihadist rams a truck into the non-Muslim guards protecting a mosque. The 7th of January, one year after the Charlie Hebdo assault, Tarek Belgacem, a Tunisian, attacked a police officer with a meat cleaver. [17] He was inspired by ISIS. In June of that year, Larossi Abballa slaughtered a police officer and his wife at their home. [18] He followed the order given by ISIS leader Abu Bakr al-Baghdadi to kill the enemy in their home during the month of Ramadan. Abballa had previously been convicted and sent to jail for recruiting jihadists to fight in Pakistan. He was released after two years. Why? Because our justice system focuses on reintegration, rather than prevention and punishment.

The 14th July 2016, the day when the French celebrate Bastille Day, another massive attack took place. Mohamed Lahouiej-Bouhiel drove a truck into the celebrating crowds in Nice. The day that celebrates the French Revolution and the conclusion of the Age of Enlightenment, saw France mourning the 86 people that were killed by a jihadist - one that clearly missed what the Age of Enlightenment was about. [15] It is sometimes said that the crucial difference in Christians and Muslims comes from the fact that Christians experienced the Enlightenment and have a rational and moderate view to their religion, as opposed to Muslims, who are said to have remained in the dark ages.

Less than two weeks later, two jihadists attack a church and kill an 86-year-old priest. Their names were

Adel Kermiche and Abdel Malik Petitjean. These two teenagers slit Jacques Hamel's throat. [14] What hatred must one hold inside to kill a peaceful priest that would meet his maker in a couple of years anyway?

The year 2017 saw another machete attack, though the guard at the Louvre was able to stop the 'Allahu Akbar' shouting jihadist before he was able to kill anyone. The perpetrator was called Abdullah Reda Refaie al-Hamahmy. [13]

In that same year Ziyed Ben Belgacem caused mayhem at the Orly airport near Paris. [12] He put a gun to the head of a soldier, but as she struggled to get away from him, he pushed her to the ground and tried to take her automatic rifle from her. While he was trying to grab the rifle, the other soldiers fired at him and killed him.

In April 2017, there was an attack carried out by Karim Cheurfi wielding an AK-47. [9] He shot dead one police officer on the Champs-Élysées. Several months later, the same famous street saw another attack. [10] This time Djaziri Adam Lotfi drove a car loaded with explosives into a police squadron. The only victim was the attacker himself. He, once more, was a self-professed jihadist. In between these two events Farid Ikken had attempted to kill a police officer with a hammer at the Notre Dame, he was arrested. [11]

Another car rammed into a group of soldiers at Levallois-Perret. The car was driven by the Islamic radical Hamou Benlatrèche, an Algerian. [6] None died, but three were severely injured. In September 2017, in

Chalon-sur-Saone, a man attacked two women wielding a hammer as a weapon once more. The attacker was shouting in Arabic and he was sought by the police in relation to his radical Islamic beliefs. [7]

In October, at the Saint-Charles train station in Marseille, Ahmed Hanachi killed two women with a knife while shouting 'Allahu Akbar'. [8] The women were twenty, and twenty-one years old, and cousins. They were called Laura Paumier and Mauranne Harel. One of them was stabbed, the other had her throat slit. Hanachi was shot dead and when he tried to attack the police.

Pictured above, the two cousins murdered by Hanachi.

Redouane Lakdim (Moroccan roots) killed four people in early 2018. Motivated by Islamic extremism, he shot and killed one person while stealing their car, only to later on kill another three people in a supermarket. A witness described him as laughing while he opened fire. [3]

Khamzat Azimov killed one person with a knife near the Paris Garnier Opera. He was already on a terrorism-watchlist. [4] In December of that year, Cherif Chekatt opened fire on people visiting a Christmas market in Strasbourg. He killed five people that had shortly before been enjoying a walk around the market. [5]

Violence continued in 2019, though it took a somewhat less prominent role in the media. In the Conde-sur-Sarthe prison a radicalized prisoner stabbed two guards, his partner had smuggled a knife into the prison for him to use during the attack. [1]

Mohamed Hichem Medjoub set off a bomb in a busy street in Lyon, though nobody died, dozens were injured. His motive was of course jihadism. [2] Mickael Harpon, born on Martinique (a small island in the Caribbean), killed four of his colleagues at the police station headquarters in Paris. His name is not clearly Islamic, but his motives were. [27]

Starting 2020, Nathan Chiasson stabbed a man to death, stabbed the man's wife in the throat, and stabbed a third person. He had also tried to stab another man, but the would-be victim explained he was a Muslim too. This was a valid reason for Nathan not to kill the man. Nathan shouted 'Allahu akbar' during the attack. [28]

Several days later, a man shouting 'Allahu akbar' tried to stab people in Metz. [29] A Sudanese refugee, motivated by Islamic beliefs, killed two people in a small place near Grenoble. He stabbed them. [30] In an attempt to take revenge for events taking place in Palestine, a man drove a car into a pair of police officers in a suburb of Paris. [31]

When Charlie Hebdo republished a few satirical cartoons, one man went to the location of their old offices, and stabbed two people on the street, seriously wounding them. [32] Some people thought this was a little funny, since the attacker was so poorly informed as to the new whereabouts of the Charlie Hebdo office. It made his entire attack look rather foolish. Yet, more than funny, it is scary that we are no longer shocked by such news.

When schoolteacher Samuel Paty showed a similar picture in his classroom, after he had offered everyone that would be offended the option to leave, a radical Islamist beheaded him. [33] Although the news of the death of Samuel Paty went viral around the world, another beheading took place a mere two weeks later in Nice. There, a radical Islamist, beheaded a woman and killed two other people. He killed them in a church, while shouting 'Allahu akbar'. [34]

At the time of writing this chapter, on the 10th of January 2021, I am not aware of any terrorist attacks taking place in France this year so far. If history teaches us anything, it will not take long before this changes. (While I am editing this, a famous director got his throat slit in front of a church a few days ago. However there is no clear statement yet on whether or not this was a terror attack, as the perpetrator is on the run. I do not want to jump to conclusions, but it sounds like it could be.)

The Research

Research done in France found that in general migrants that are unemployed commit more crime, than natives that are unemployed. They also claim that when comparing for economic situation for the employed immigrants, the crime rates are similar. [35] That sounds positive, until we read on Statista that 'In 2007, more than 14 percent of immigrants were jobless in France, compared to 7 percent of the non-immigrant population. More than ten years later, in 2018, the share of people looking for a job in France amounted to 8.3 percent for non-immigrants and reached 15.3 percent for immigrants.' [36] So in other words, immigrants are twice as likely to be unemployed. For women from outside of the EU, the percentage that is unemployed sits at 26%, while for French women it is only 8%. This hints at the fact that immigrants from outside of the European Union are even more likely to be unemployed. Thus, that 15.3% of the overall immigrant population that is unemployed may be higher for non-EU immigrants, and very likely is when we assume that the difference between non-EU men and women is not significant. Plus the effect on crime rate may be higher for the non-EU immigrants, as this also wasn't split when reviewing the crime statistics.

Besides that, it is obvious that not the entire group will engage in criminal behavior. Those most likely to be criminals, are those most likely to be unemployed. A jihadist has no desire to be a valuable contributor to society. Despite the writers of the research attempting to sell it as a positive, with 'only' a difference of crime rate for the unemployed, they ignore that the portion of unemployed immigrants is relatively larger, and more criminal. So as a group, on average, immigrants are overrepresented in crime statistics, though the large group of unemployed immigrants carries it. A letdown on the research is that it does not split EU and non-EU immigrants, even though other countries show us that such differences are critical. Moreover, it does not seem to acknowledge the immigrants that have since acquired a French passport, as well as their offspring.

Paris

The situation in Paris can be no surprise. 'According to alarming new statistics, 47.6 percent of criminals in certain departments of Paris are foreign-born'. [37] Paris is overrun. The bill that prevents people from recording police during their work, was related to the police cleaning up a migrant camp in the middle of the city. Obviously 'bad press', it shows that the French government is struggling to deal with a very real problem, while maintaining a kind face. [38]

Once a lovely city, full of beauty and romance, Paris has degraded. Visitors to Paris today feel unsafe, and are afraid of leaving the touristic heart of the city. There, accompanied by soldiers armed with machine guns, people can enjoy the sights and history that the city has to offer. Leave the heart of the city, and an odd feeling comes over you. That feeling is not misplaced.

The Parisian suburbs, full of immigrants, are also full of unrest. Rioters do not refrain from launching fireworks at the police. [39] Also let us not forget that time in 2019 where Congolese rioters burned down dozens of cars, because a Congolese artist was allowed to perform in the area. They did not support this particular Congolese artist. [40] Burning cars seems to be the solution to everything, according to those living in the Parisian suburbs. And who lives in those suburbs? Well, frankly, immigrants do. Including up to 400.000 illegal immigrants. For the most part, the cars they burn are their own. [41]

In another instance, a migrant youth died in a traffic accident. Despite there being no indication of police involvement, migrants living in the area for some reason decided it was the police's fault anyway, and began to riot. Burning cars, fireworks launched at the police, the usual. [42]

Burning Cars

Some argue that the habit of burning cars during a protest is quintessentially French. That, however, begs the question. Although news outlets are careful not to blame migrants, all evidence does point into their direction. The habit of burning cars did not start until the 1990's, after the first wave of immigrants had entered and settled in. The habit is most popular in cities like Paris and Marseille, cities with large immigrant populations. Within those cities, it takes place in the suburbs, where the migrants live. And if that doesn't quite convince you, there is the example of the African Cup of Nations. The government refused to publish how many cars were burned during the semifinals on the 14th of July, fearing that it would spark a challenge to the perpetrators to burn even more cars during the finals on the 19th of July. Apparently burning cars is a great way to either celebrate your home country's victory in a football game, or to mourn your loss. [43]

And yes, there are other sources that do admit it is an immigrant problem. [45] 'The custom of setting vehicles alight on New Year's Eve is set to have kicked off around Strasbourg, eastern France in the 1990s, in the city's deprived, high-immigrant districts.' Most websites leave the part of 'high-immigrant districts' out when they describe how it started in Strasbourg. Nobody wants to appear xenophobic.

Don't forget - anything is a good reason to burn cars. So when the French police executed the law, and gave a woman a fine for wearing a face veil, the result was to be expected. Cars were, indeed, burned. [44]

French Prisons

With such crime statistics, it is not strange to see it reflected in the statistics of prison inmates. France, believing in the blank slate, everyone being born equal, does not gather statistics on race, religion, or origin. Thereby, it can be difficult to assess the percentage of immigrants in French prisons too. Still, if we go by the percentage of prisoners that registers for Ramadan, we already reach 27%. [46]

That number is expected to be an underrepresentation of Muslims, as some Muslims do not care to register, or are afraid to be spotted as religious Muslims by intelligence agencies. Estimations sit between 40% and 70% of actual Muslim inmates. That, despite Muslims forming around 6-8% of the French population, hence a huge overrepresentation.

Here, we must note that the Muslims are not the only immigrants in French prisons. France also has a significant number of Christian immigrants from Africa or Eastern Europe. We can only guess what the total percentage of immigrants in French prisons becomes, but it is clearly high.

Civil War in Dijon

Let us not forget the time when Dijon, the capital city of Burgundy, flared up in the summer of 2020. After Algerians had assaulted a Chechen teenager in an apparent drug turf war, the Chechens decided to launch an attack on the Maghreb-run gangs in the city. Now, when we say 'assault', what we mean is that they put a gun to his head and threatened him.

For multiple days, dozens of Chechen foot soldiers walked through the suburbs of Dijon, weapons in hand. The local police were not equipped to handle the situation, but it took days before a serious response was organized on the national level. During that time, the suburbs were effectively under the control of the Chechen mafia. It is believed that the Chechens descended upon Dijon not only from other areas of France, but Belgium, the Netherlands, and Germany as well. A true international crime network. [48]

'Myth Detector'

Some people seek to remain blind for the events taking place right in front of their eyes. And some writers wish to argue that migrants really are not the cause of crime in a country such as France. [47]

This article on 'myth detector' is such an attempt. One of the points they make is that non-citizens, so the recently arrived immigrants that do not yet have a French passport, are not responsible for the majority of the crime. No, they argue, it is the French citizens that are responsible for 84% of crime. A great statistic, but meaningless. French citizens formed 94% of the French population. This means that the 6% of the population that were non-citizens were responsible for 16% of the crime. In other words, these newly arrived immigrants are far more criminal than the French citizens are! And beyond that, that 94%, which forms the French citizens, that includes a large group of immigrants that have acquired French citizenship after living in France for a few years, as well as their children. We will see that second-generation immigrants can be even more criminal than their parents. The percentage of crimes committed by the ethnic French is not discussed. In fact, this myth busting article has only succeeded in showing that the newly arrived immigrants are indeed more criminal, and a danger to French society.

In the article's last attempt to defend the Syrian and Iraqi immigrants in France, it highlights that these groups are not as criminal as those from other countries are. They show that immigrants from Algeria, Tunisia, and Morocco, to name a few, are in fact responsible for more crimes, when looking at sexual misconduct and murder. But what does that prove? Does it prove immigration does not push up crime? No, it only shows that Algerians, Tunisians, and Moroccans do commit a lot of crime. At best, the comparison shows that some immigrants are even less desirable than others are. I doubt that is the point the author of the article wished to make. Unless the goal was to close the borders with the Maghreb specifically.

Summary

To summarize, France sees an immense rate of Islamic terrorist attacks, with severe casualties. It has frequent riots, mobs attacking the police, or groups burning cars either to celebrate or to complain. Migrants are overrepresented in all forms of crime, a difference that cannot be explained away by socio-economic status. Which, in turn, brings about a massive, though still vague, overrepresentation of immigrants in French prisons. Paris, once the city of romance and love, has turned into a city of violence and fear.

"I have tried to lift France out of the mud. But she will return to her errors and vomiting. I cannot prevent the French from being French."

- Charles de Gaulle

Notes:

[1] https://www.dw.com/en/terror-probe-launched-after-french-prisoner-stabs-guards/a-47786761

[2] https://www.newsweek.com/lyon-bomb-attack-terror-injuries-casualties-france-1435781

[3] https://www.theguardian.com/world/2018/mar/24/france-supermarket-gunman-radouane-lakdim-what-we-know-so-far

[4] https://www.independent.co.uk/news/world/europe/khamzat-azimov-paris-attack-stabbing-knife-kill-terror-chechen-chechnya-edited-a8351071.html

[5] https://www.telegraaf.nl/nieuws/2908613/kerstmarktschutter-chekatt-29-heeft-behoorlijk-strafblad

[6] https://www.theguardian.com/world/2017/aug/10/paris-police-wait-to-interview-suspect-after-car-rammed-soldiers

[7] https://www.mirror.co.uk/news/world-news/chalon-sur-sane-hammer-attack-11177873

[8] https://www.thetimes.co.uk/article/marseilles-killer-ahmed-hanachi-should-have-been-deported-macron-mauranne-harel-laura-paumier-mjqhvwnj6

[9]   https://www.bbc.com/news/world-europe-39671542

[10]   https://guardian.ng/news/world/car-ploughs-into-police-van-in-paris-champs-elysees-attack/

[11]   https://www.en24news.com/2020/10/farid-ikken-sentenced-to-twenty-eight-years-in-prison.html

[12] https://www.theguardian.com/world/2017/mar/18/paris-airport-attacker-had-long-criminal-record

[13]   https://www.cbsnews.com/news/louvre-museum-attack-paris-egyptian-not-talking-father-speaks/

[14]   https://www.kn.nl/nieuws/priester-jacques-hamel-ik-werk-tot-mijn-laatste-adem/

[15]   https://www.timesofisrael.com/france-arrests-8-over-july-truck-attack-that-killed-86-in-nice/

[16] https://edition.cnn.com/2015/01/21/europe/2015-paris-terror-attacks-fast-facts/index.html

[17]   https://www.hln.be/default/dader-parijs-geidentificeerd-als-tunesier-tarek-belgacem~a3372f4a/

[18]   https://www.bbc.com/news/world-europe-36526067

[19]   https://www.bbc.com/news/uk-england-essex-54825879

[20]
https://www.telegraph.co.uk/news/worldnews/europe/france/11701172/Yacine-Sali-Everything-we-know-about-the-suspected-Grenoble-attacker.html

[21]
https://www.telegraaf.nl/nieuws/243477956/levenslang-voor-thalys-terrorist-ayoub-el-khazzani

[22]   https://www.bbc.com/news/world-europe-17456541

[23]
https://www.express.co.uk/news/world/1302942/paris-la-defense-station-gunman-france-terror-armed-police

[24]   https://www.france24.com/en/20141221-police-shooting-allahu-akbar-joue-tours-jihad-islamic-state

[25]   https://www.bbc.com/news/world-europe-31118020

[26]
https://www.breitbart.com/europe/2020/11/06/france-algerian-jailed-for-killing-a-woman-and-trying-to-bomb-a-church-in-paris/

[27]   https://www.bbc.com/news/world-europe-49931153

[28]   https://www.mirror.co.uk/news/world-news/breaking-villejuif-incident-paris-police-21207373

[29] https://www.reuters.com/article/us-france-security/french-police-shoot-and-wound-knifeman-shouting-allahu-akbar-in-metz-idUSKBN1Z40ON

[30] https://www.bbc.com/news/world-europe-52165522

[31] https://www.france24.com/en/20200428-driver-rams-two-police-motorcyclists-in-paris-suburb

[32] https://apnews.com/article/paris-archive-72e7b2b35da5a8472935bdd738f19dea?utm_campaign=SocialFlow&utm_medium=AP&utm_source=Twitter

[33] https://www.bbc.com/news/world-europe-54573356

[34] https://www.reuters.com/article/us-france-security-nice/two-dead-in-knife-attack-in-french-church-official-say-terrorism-suspected-idUSKBN27E17D

[35] Yu Aoki & Yasuyuki Todo (2009) Are immigrants more likely to commit crimes? Evidence from France, Applied Economics Letters, 16:15, 1537-1541, DOI: 10.1080/13504850701578892

[36] https://www.statista.com/statistics/761176/jobseekers-immigration-status-france/

[37] https://rmx.news/article/article/nearly-half-of-paris-ghetto-criminals-have-a-migrant-background

[38]   https://www.bbc.com/news/world-europe-55055914

[39] https://www.express.co.uk/news/world/1272566/emmanuel-macron-news-protest-riots-france-coronavirus-latest-lockdown-paris-riot-police

[40]   https://www.eutimes.net/2020/03/congolese-migrants-riot-in-paris-set-fire-to-dozens-of-vehicles/

[41] https://www.telegraph.co.uk/news/2018/07/05/illegal-migrants-paris-suburb-soar-400000-hundreds-migrant-children/

[42] https://summit.news/2020/05/21/migrants-riot-for-fourth-consecutive-night-in-paris/

[43]   https://freewestmedia.com/2019/07/16/hiding-the-number-of-cars-burned-in-france-during-can-celebrations/

[44]   https://www.ynetnews.com/articles/0,7340,L-4407897,00.html

[45] https://www.telegraph.co.uk/news/2017/01/02/almost-1000-cars-torched-around-france-new-years-eve-government/

[46]   https://www.adamsmith.org/blog/are-70-of-frances-prison-inmates-muslims

[47]
https://www.mythdetector.ge/en/myth/disinformatio
n-number-crimes-committed-immigrants-france-and-
germany-increases

[48]   https://www.volkskrant.nl/nieuws-
achtergrond/tsjetsjenen-op-strafexpeditie-tegen-
maghrebbijnse-jongeren-in-dijon~bf239513/

Belgian Bastards

"Belgium is a country invented by the British to annoy the French."

- Charles de Gaulle

Belgium, squeezed in between the Netherlands and France, is multicultural from the start. The Flemish north speaks Dutch, while the Walloons in the south speak French. Despite existing for nearly two centuries, that division is still a topic of hot debate. The arrival of non-Western immigrants only complicates things.

Adil and Ibrahim

In Belgium we see some similarity with France. When a youth named 'Adil' crashed his scooter into a police van and died, this led to a small riot where a police van was demolished with stones and pallets thrown at it. [1]

In 2021 a twenty three-year-old called Ibrahim died after being arrested by the police. Protestors claimed he was killed by the police for being black. Riots broke out, fires were started, and police officers were attacked. The police officers got beaten up, and escaped with their lives. [7]

Terrorism

Islamic terrorism is no stranger to Belgium either. The greatest attack was a twin bombing that took place in 2016. Both a metro station and the Zaventem Airport were attacked - thirty-two people were killed. The year saw further stabbings of police agents. In 2017 we saw a bombing in Brussels Central Station, perpetrated by a Moroccan. Later that year a man attacked people with a machete. Then, in 2018, an escaped convict killed three people. ISIS claimed responsibility for the attacks. [8]

Brussels

Brussels, the capital, has degraded. An opinion article in the Guardian writes, 'Among Belgians, Brussels has something of a reputation for being an unsafe city where criminals of Moroccan and other immigrant extractions rule its mean streets and certain neighborhoods are no-go areas, not only for law-abiding citizens but also for the police. Three recent incidents, including a dramatic one in which a police officer was shot with a Kalashnikov during a getaway after a thwarted armed robbery, have confirmed this perception.' [2]

Statistics

In Belgium, it is not easy to find statistics on crime data. Even an article that confirms Moroccans are overrepresented in Belgian crime data, is eager to show that these findings should not be used to make judgements. [3] In a hilariously odd comparison, near the end of the article it shows us how great North-Africans really are, by stating that the Roman Emperor Severus was of North-African origins. Not only that, but they continue to say that diversity was a strength for the Roman Empire, and it was the barbaric Germans that caused its decline. It is worth highlighting here that the author of the article is called Fouad Gandoul, a seemingly North-African name. Somehow, his logic holds that immigration into the Roman Empire by North-Africans was good, but immigration by the Germanic barbarians was bad.

Factual data on Belgian migrant crime is hard to come by. Dutch scientists even complain about the lack of data in Belgium, which makes any kind of research near impossible. [6] The statistics that are available, don't look good for migrants. One out of three people arrested in Belgium, does not have Belgian citizenship. Again, this does not even include immigrants that have acquired a Belgian passport, nor their children. [4] Around one in seven is a non-European foreigner. Now if these numbers don't sound bad enough, it's because they're not adjusted for the per capita presence of such foreigners. Adjusted for that, it turns out non-European migrants are six times more likely to be suspected of having committed a crime, than Belgians. A very significant difference. [5]

"Truth seldom finds a home."

– Belgian proverb

Notes:

[1]   https://summit.news/2020/04/13/migrant-youths-riot-in-belgium-despite-coronavirus-lockdown/

[2] https://www.theguardian.com/commentisfree/2010/feb/08/brussels-crime-police-unemployment

[3]   https://www.knack.be/nieuws/belgie/belgische-marokkanen-in-de-criminaliteitscijfers-de-statistieken-vertellen-niet-alles/article-opinion-561261.html?cookie_check=1610825176

[4]   https://www.hln.be/binnenland/nieuwe-criminaliteitscijfers-van-politie-1-op-3-verdachten-is-buitenlander~a1c0bfc2/

[5]   https://www.vlaamsbelang.org/criminaliteit-europeanen-6-maal-hoger-dan-belgen/

[6] https://www.demorgen.be/nieuws/wetenschappers-hekelen-gebrek-aan-cijfers-over-migratieachtergrond-en-crimineel-gedrag~b40dd3fe/?referrer=https%3A%2F%2Fwww.google.nl%2F

[7]   https://www.hln.be/brussel/betoging-voor-overleden-ibrahima-23-ontspoort-volledig-meer-dan-100-arrestaties-relschoppers-bekogelen-politiekantoor-met-molotovcocktails~aab0f60e/

[8]   https://www.bbc.com/news/av/world-europe-35869177

ILLEGAL IN ITALY

"You may have the universe if I may have Italy."

- *Giuseppe Verdi*

The once mighty Roman Empire, long fallen and erected several times since. Now, the city states of the Italian peninsula have once more united to form a nation. Walking through Rome, through Venice, through Florence, you can feel the history. If Europe is the body, then Italy is the heart.

The Research Done

Studies have shown varying results in Italy, although all of them show some sort of increase in crime connected to migrants. A study done on immigrant crime in Italy between 1990 and 2003 found that immigrants only increase the frequency of robberies. [1] Another study found that Italian towns with a higher percentage of migrants, also allocate more funds to their police departments. [2] What is not clear from the study is whether this is a response to an increase in crime, or a pre-emptive move due to fears that migrants will cause crime and a lower sense of security. Then another study was done, which did not show an increase in robbery, but did show an increase in sexual exploitation. [3] The study also argued that migrants could be replacing the native criminals from crimes such as drug dealing. Not unlikely, as it appears the infamous Italian crime families may have moved into the trade of smuggling refugees into the country. [4]

Nevertheless, aggregate data shows a different story. In 2011, 43% of people entering prison were immigrants. Immigrants were highly overrepresented in convictions, with 25% of people convicted being immigrants, despite the immigrant population at the time sitting around 6-7%. Keep in mind, all these numbers are from before the great migrant movements that started in 2015. [5] Moreover, it shows that these immigrants did not come from other EU member states. They had arrived from Africa for the most part, and additionally a smaller segment coming from non-EU Eastern Europe. It is not a great leap to implicate the Sinti coming from Romania and Bulgaria for a portion of these criminals.

Such statistics were matched by a statement in 2018, which confirmed that immigrants were suspected of 31.9% of the crimes in Italy. [6] Despite, still, only forming around 8% of the population. The percentage is, moreover, on an increasing trend. It is nonetheless shocking, one in three crimes could have been prevented by keeping the borders closed.

Also when it comes to rape, migrants are overrepresented. It is said that migrants only commit 10% of all rapes, which is an overrepresentation in its own right, but it may be far worse than that. Nearly 70% of all rapes are said to be committed by the victim's partner. Unfortunately, the statistics do not differentiate between stranger rape, and partner rape. Although all rape may be a traumatic experience, it is fair to judge that stranger rape leads to greater trauma than partner rape. Only 30% of rapes were not partner rape. If we were to hypothesize that the migrants are always suspected of non-partner rape, their share would rise to one in three. One in three non-partner rapes may be perpetrated by migrants. Likewise, the percentage could be zero, if all migrants only commit rape on their partners. That, however, seems unlikely. In all honesty, we are left guessing due to a lack of proper data. [7]

For every 1% population increase of migrants living in an area, the crime rate goes up by 0.4%. That is a direct clearly causal relationship between migrants and crime. [8] On top of that, legal immigrants are twice as likely to be convicted compared to the native Italians. Illegal immigrants are more than ten times as likely to be convicted, compared to the native Italians. The implication is that a town that consists solely of immigrants, legal immigrants, will still have a crime rate that is twice as high as compared to a town that consists solely of native Italians. The effect is so strong, that the north of Italy now has more problems with crime, than the infamous south.

Google's Bias

On a side-note, it is shocking how biased the mainstream media are when it comes to reporting news. When you search Google for migrant crime, your first page is going to be filled with articles detailing how 'racists' have attacked migrants. So-called anti-migrant crime. These articles include pictures, detailed narratives, and individual stories. These same newspapers refuse to report crimes perpetrated by migrants on the natives in the same way. As if such crimes do not exist. Luckily, the data does not lie, so they cannot hide it completely. Yet, if all you read is a newspaper like 'The Guardian', you will believe migrants are the poor victims, while Italians are always the ones attacking innocent immigrants. Sure, from time to time such newspapers like the Guardian have interesting and fair articles, but the bias persists.

The bias applies to Google itself as well. Looking for articles on such politically incorrect topics, the results on Google are very different than they are on a search engine like Bing or Ecosia. Google, it seems, has modified the results for such topics to present a clear politically correct bias on the first page. Due to the near monopoly position Google has, this gives it all a very '1984' kind of vibe.

The Mafia and the Nigerians

The mafia appears to have accepted cooperation with the African newcomers back in 2017. Nigerian gangs and the traditional mafia cooperate when it comes to people smuggling, prostitution rings, and the heroin trade. [9] The Nigerians are not simple thugs, but form organized criminality. Under names such as 'The Vikings' or 'Black Axe' they operate throughout Europe.

One of their activities consists of bringing Nigerian girls and women into Europe, where they are forced into prostitution. (We saw the same gangs active in Ireland.) Selling their body for as little as five or ten euro, they have to pay off debts that go up to sixty-thousand euro. In practice, the Italian mafia, the NGO's (Non-Governmental Organizations) that pick up the migrants in front of the coast in Libya, and the Nigerian mob all work together in order for Nigerian girls to sell their bodies. The girls are coerced to work in one part because their documents are taken away from them, but also because of African black magic. They believe a curse will get to them or their family if they are not obedient. [10]

It is not an easy problem for the Italian police. Besides not knowing much about the Nigerians, one gang easily replaces another. A successful bust of the Vikings, has only given the Black Axe an opportunity to take their place. [11] The Nigerians are in some instances starting to grow stronger than the original Italian mafia. Their focus sits on trading women, cocaine, and heroin. Women from Africa, cocaine from South-America, and heroin from Asia. All of it goes to Italy, and from there to the rest of Europe. A truly global network. During a period where Italy was gaining the upper hand on their homegrown mafia, they are now facing this new threat.

The Nigerians don't have a great reputation in Italy, which is impacted by other kinds of crime coming to light too. [12] A Nigerian drug dealer was convicted for the murder of an Italian teenage girl. The girl had been cut into pieces. Crimes such as these have led to acts of vengeance on the Nigerian community in Italy, where Nigerians have been targeted by the Italians. More or less a slow-moving low-profile race war. [13]

Rape

The most high profile rape case in Italy comes in the form of a gang rape of a Polish tourist. She was walking along the beach with her boyfriend, when a Congolese man, two underage Moroccans, and an underage Nigerian attacked them. The girl was raped in front of her boyfriend. Additionally, they were mugged. [14]

We can see that the statistics show that migrants increase crime, and violent crime, in Italy. They are overrepresented in the rape category. They are taking over organized crime. And more and more keep arriving every day.

"What is the fatal charm of Italy? What do we find there that can be found nowhere else? I believe it is a certain permission to be human, which other places, other countries, lost long ago."

– Erica Jong

Notes:

[1] https://academic.oup.com/jeea/article-abstract/10/6/1318/2299419?redirectedFrom=PDF

[2] https://voxeu.org/article/immigration-fear-and-public-spending-security

[3] http://www.rassegnaitalianadicriminologia.it/en/home/item/61-limpatto-dellimmigrazione-sulla-delinquenza-una-verifica-dellipotesi-della-sostituzione-nellitalia-degli-anni-90

[4] https://www.theguardian.com/news/2018/feb/01/migrants-more-profitable-than-drugs-how-mafia-infiltrated-italy-asylum-system

[5] https://web.archive.org/web/20160202205357/http://www.frdb.org/upload/file/Report%201.pdf

[6] https://www.breitbart.com/europe/2018/08/25/nearly-one-three-crimes-italy-committed-foreigners/

[7] https://islamineurope.blogspot.com/2007/12/italy-immigrants-turn-to-crime-due-to.html

[8] https://www.breitbart.com/europe/2016/11/23/italy-report-immigrants-crime/

[9]
https://www.breitbart.com/europe/2017/06/28/italy
-mafia-migrant-gangs-running-heroin-prostitution-
rings-together/

[10]   https://www.abc.net.au/news/2020-03-
17/castel-volturno-is-headquarters-for-nigerian-mafia-
in-italy/12033684

[11]   https://www.occrp.org/en/daily/13348-italy-
arrests-dozens-of-suspected-nigerian-mafia-members

[12]
https://www.breitbart.com/europe/2019/05/31/nige
rian-migrant-sentenced-life-murder-italian-teen/

[13]   https://nypost.com/2018/02/03/italian-
gunman-targeted-immigrants-after-nigerian-man-was-
arrested-for-killing/

[14]   https://www.reuters.com/article/us-italy-rapes-
idUSKCN1BO23C

GANG RAPE IN GERMANY

"Germany is a great nation only because its people have so much Polish blood in their veins."

- Friedrich Nietzsche

Germany, the Teutonic land. Twice they tried to conquer Europe, twice they lost. The rape conducted by Russian soldiers invading Berlin in 1945 was a one-off. Now, the Germans are under constant attack.

Cologne

Migrant crime in Germany rose to prominence in early 2016, when it became apparent that during the New Year's celebrations in Cologne and lesser-known Hamburg, huge masses of young migrant men had sexually assaulted more than a thousand young German women. [11]

By July 2016, only four of these men had been convicted. Two of those had arrived in Germany only recently, forming a part of the major migration movement of 2015.

The Correspondent gives us this depiction of the events, "It's New Year's Eve, an hour past midnight. Kirsten is inside Cologne's main train station, hemmed in by a big crowd. She's trying to reach the stairs to the platform, but she can't move. It's noisy, and the air stinks of alcohol and sweat. Kirsten gasps for air. Suddenly she feels a hand sliding across her buttocks, under her skirt. She pushes it away. The building is so crowded, she can't tell who's groped her. A few minutes later, the same thing happens again. She feels trapped and powerless.

Meanwhile, Yousef Aljork is standing outside the station, below the iconic clock towers of Cologne's Gothic cathedral. The square between the station and the cathedral is packed, mostly with young men waving beer bottles. The bang of exploding firecrackers is everywhere. Aljork sees a group of men surrounding a woman and grabbing her. He's close enough to hear the men speaking Arabic." If the races had been reversed, it would've been named a hate crime. Hordes of Arab men that harass German girls. "Around midnight, things took a turn for the worse," Aljork says. "Some men trapped one or two women between them and started touching them all over. Some of them were stealing money, phones, or other things."

Kirsten continues, "First, I felt something on my buttocks, and I thought, What's that?" she says. "I tried to push it away, and then I realized it was a hand. But it was so crowded, I couldn't even tell who was touching me. A few minutes later, the same thing happened again, but this time, a hand touched me right on the genitals. It wasn't accidental. It went under my skirt, and that was deliberate. Somebody really groped me."

Now some migrant apologists will say that German men also grope women in the disco, and without saying that that's okay, are we sure we can compare those behaviors? There is a difference in a drunk, creepy, guy touching your ass, that you can respond to with disgust, slap, and continue partying without needing to be afraid, and being stuck between a group of men all purposefully touching you, not just on your ass, but going straight for your genitals, reaching under your skirt - multiple men, multiple times - while at the same time stealing your wallet and phone. [12]

In a hilarious perversion of justice, The Correspondent casts doubt on 'what really happened that night', based on the fact that other witnesses that were present in Cologne that night did not see anyone being groped. Now, first of all, it is hard to see if someone is being groped when they are surrounded by a horde of men. Second, that a witness did not see something does not hold up as evidence of innocence in any court of law. If I commit burglary, and the neighbor says he did not see me steal the jewelry, that is no reason to then claim that there is insufficient evidence, when the other neighbor does admit to seeing me steal the jewelry. The logic there makes no sense! It is not the case that these other witnesses are saying the supposed perpetrators have a great alibi, all they say is that they personally did not see it. But, it's not even clear if they were still in that area at the time of the crime being committed.

The desire to sow doubt on migrants actually being criminal in the media is insane and forces them to avoid all logic. Do they claim those hundreds of women that went to the police to report these crimes lied? Hundreds of women that, without any coordinator, communication, or even common goal, all went to the police, are supposed to be an unreliable source that something indeed did happen. To claim that we cannot be sure, and that we need to doubt that something wrong took place that night, is a horrible slap in the face to the victims.

The BBC Fact Check

The BBC has an interesting article on crime in Germany, a fact check. The leader of the AfD, Alternative fur Deutschland, stated that there had been 447 murders and killings by illegal migrants on Germans. The fact check confirmed that this statement was false - the 447 referred to murder and attempted murder or killing, done by asylum seekers and refugees; legal and illegal. However, whether the migrants are legal or illegal is not relevant for our hypothesis that migrants do indeed drive up crime, and make life less pleasant.

The article has curious writing such as 'Then, on 9 September, there were rival far-right and left-wing demonstrations in Köthen, also in eastern Germany, after a German man died in an incident involving Afghan men." An incident involving Afghan men is surely a strange way of saying the German man was killed or murdered by a group of Afghan men. He didn't die in a car accident, it wasn't a cruel twist of fate – he was murdered.

The BBC actually admits that the inflow of migrants has had a strong enough effect on crime in

Germany to end a long downward crime trend. "Bar a blip in the mid-2000s, overall crime has been decreasing in Germany since the early 1990s. But that changed in 2015 - about the same time hundreds of thousands of refugees began entering the country." The article continues, "Within that, violent crime rose from 180,000 cases to 193,000 between 2014 and 2016. The number of murders increased by 14.6% and rapes by 8%, over the same period." So yes, the inflow of migrants caused an end to the downward crime trend and reversed it.

"The AfD has made claims about a link between the influx of migrants and a rise in crime. Since 2014, the proportion of non-German suspects in the crime statistics has increased from 24% to just over 30% (when we take out crimes related to immigration and asylum irregularities). Breaking that down even further, in 2017 those classified as "asylum applicants or civil war refugees or illegal immigrants" represented a total of 8.5% of all suspects. This is despite their population representing just 2% of Germany as a whole." Again, why do they say the AfD has made 'claims'? Clearly, what the AfD has said is true and based on facts. They even confirm the facts in their own article. The truth is right in front of them, but their self-censorship prevents them from admitting the reality around them.

Asylum seekers in the national crime picture
% of asylum seeker suspects vs proportion of population

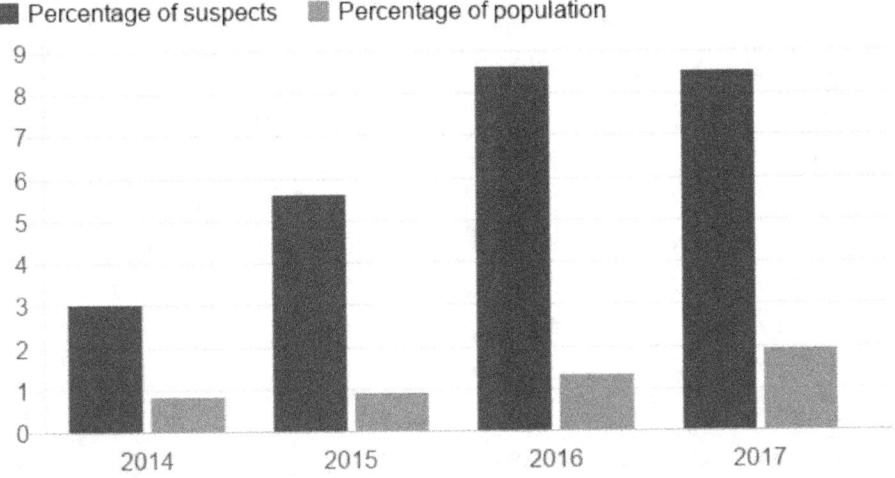

Source: BKA, asylum seekers defined as "asylum applicants, quota or civil war refugees or irregular immigrants"; figures exclude immigration and asylum irregularity offences

Of course, the BBC will not say that the immigrants are to blame for their criminal conduct. Besides the demographics of the immigrant group being predominantly young men, and young men are known to commit more crime, they also say this, 'They have social deprivation, they are alone and they spend most of their time with other people suffering from these risk factors - the accommodation of the majority of asylum seekers is like refugee camps with little privacy, which again can add to the likelihood of committing crimes.' [2]

Now first off, when the migrant caravan marched through Europe, the media wanted to emphasize how these were vulnerable people. Women, children, the elderly. Right-wing media that claimed it was mostly young, military-age men, were seen as provocative and racist.

Snopes even 'debunked' the claim that the migrants were mostly young men, and stated it was 'mostly false'. [1] Clearly, either Snopes, or the BBC article is wrong. If the BBC is wrong, then the demographics form no foundation for the increase in crime whatsoever - at least not demographics with regards to age. If Snopes is wrong, then the question becomes why we are so eager to welcome these migrants, when they are clearly not the most vulnerable. No, the most vulnerable would be the ones that remain in the migrant camps in Jordan, Syria, and Lebanon.

Second, the BBC gives reasons such as 'social deprivation' and 'little privacy'. These can, somehow, apparently, increase the likelihood of committing crimes. Frankly, I am not sure how this causal relationship would work. Half the world is currently socially deprived due to lockdown measures in place, should we expect crime statistics to jump upwards in 2020? And not just domestic violence, no, crimes such as rape and murder.

How would social deprivation motivate a person to rape or kill? How would living with little privacy bring about such behavior? Nor does it explain the effect on crime of second-generation immigrants, who do not suffer from any of these deprivations. The logic is simply missing in the BBC article, but it is the BBC, so they cannot admit a simple fact; migrants bring crime.

Does the media focus on migrant crime?

Rather than making such admissions, the question is raised whether news broadcasters don't focus too much on migrant crime. This discussion flared up again after an Eritrean man pushed a mother and her eight-year-old son in front of a train in Frankfurt. Because, they argued, it wasn't broadcasted as wide when a German man had attacked an Eritrean man a week earlier. The Eritrean man was shot at by a man who is supposed to have far-right sympathies, but survived. [3]

Perhaps we should consider that the news of a mother and son being pushed, randomly, in front of a train is simply more shocking to us. Perhaps the absolute cold-bloodedness and needlessness of the crime is what made it so newsworthy, so much talked about. Because, who would do such a thing?

The Eritrean man who was shot by a German, was a supposedly racially motivated crime, if a personal link existed remains unclear. The police claim racism is the case because the perpetrator was white, and the victim black. They could not check with the attacker, because he shot himself afterwards.

However, when the Eritrean man pushed the mother and son in front of the train, nobody talked about it being anti-white racism. They only said that it happened. And why shouldn't they? Isn't such a nightmare scenario taking place in real life a newsworthy event?

There's Data...

For Germany, we have even more data available. 'While making up only 12 percent of the population, the proportion of foreigners among criminal suspects was 37 percent. In the case of murder, that proportion was even higher, with nearly 40 percent of suspects listed as "immigrants". Germany also saw an increase in sexual crimes in 2019, with 8,189 suspects listed as "non-German", representing more than one in three sexual crimes (36 percent).'

Twelve percent of the population causes more than one-third of the crime. [4] Not only that, but the violence also appears to be very one-sided. Migrants commit crimes against Germans, while Germans rarely commit crimes against migrants; 'in the category of "sexual offenses", 3,261 Germans were victims in sexual crimes featuring an immigrant as the suspect while only 89 immigrants were victims of a German suspect.'

More than three thousand Germans were victims of this 12%, while less than a hundred immigrants faced a German perpetrator. If the perpetrators and victims were randomly distributed, this would not occur. The data instead implies that more violent immigrants are actively seeking out German victims, while Germans show no particular interest in immigrants.

'The Federal **Criminal Police Office's (BKA) first quarter report for 2019 also showed** that as a group, refugees, asylum seekers and individuals with no German residency who can't be deported, known as *Geduldete* in German, are the most overrepresented group featuring criminal suspects in all of Germany. With the majority of this group arriving in 2015 or later, they represented only 2 percent of the German population but accounted for 15 percent of cases of deadly violence and 12 percent of rape or sexual assault suspects.'

Is it then fair to ask why the opponents of Merkel's open-border policy were ridiculed for saying the migrants would bring crime? A government ought to protect its own people, but it seems the German government could have done a much better job at that.

These statistics do not give us further detail, nor do they seem to include second-generation immigrants, as these are simply considered German.

EU Fact Check

Despite all this data, the EU Fact Check website still denies an increase in crime caused by immigrants, applying some dubious logic. [9]

They check the claim made by Donald Trump that crime in Germany increased by 10% since the flow of migrants arrived. Now, I admit, this claim is not accurate for crime in general. Which, in turn, is due to crime having been on a downward trend. Murder, homicide, and manslaughter, however, did increase by just over 10%.

Why does the article say Trump's claim is wrong? Because this increase of 10% included all victims from the terror attack in Berlin when a truck drove through a Christmas market. Somehow, in their logic it is unfair to include mass-murder in murder statistics. Even so, it does not make the conclusion that murder increased by 10% according to German data false. Those people were killed by someone, why shouldn't their deaths matter? It seems to be an arbitrary separation in order to fit the idea that migrants do not bring more crime.

When we look at sexual crimes, we see an increase of 40%. However, they say there was a change in the law during this time that expanded the definition of 'rape'. Such a change in the definition on rape can indeed expand the amount of rape cases.

They make no effort to check whether that legal change explains the full 40% or if it is only a partial explanation. There is no evidence to conclude that the 40% rise was exclusively due to the change in the law, or if any of it was due to the change in the law. We simply cannot conclude anything here.

Therefore, they conclude Trump's claim was 'mostly false'. Still, when we wish to see if migrants cause crime, we can also just check their overrepresentation in crime data, which we have done before, and continue to do for other countries. Everywhere, statistics show migrants are overrepresented.

The problem then with these 'fact checks' is that they don't really check any facts at all, and if they do, they twist and turn their conclusions to fit their agenda. In essence, they become fake news. They are that which they claim to counter. Their own enemy.

What about the youth?

When it comes to refugee children, policies around Europe are always more relaxed. Now despite it being apparent that many immigrants lie about their age, age does not seem to be a barrier for crime. [5]

A seventeen-year-old refugee from Afghanistan raped and murdered a German girl. Another Afghan boy, this time only fifteen years old, stabbed his ex-girlfriend in the heart in the middle of a shop. [6]

Proper statistics on such crimes are hard to find, but similar news articles seem to pop up frequently. How often does it happen that a teenage German boy stabs his ex-girlfriend to death in the middle of a shop? Do you believe it would not make the front page, because it is such a dull story? Alternatively, is it not on the front page, because it does not happen?

Susanna

Then there is the heart-breaking story of Susanna, a fifteen-year-old Jewish girl. [7] Born to a Jewish mother and Kurdish father, she was raised by a single mother. Susanna fell in love with a refugee boy, the same age as her. From kindergarten onwards, she had been taught to befriend people from other cultures. That is exactly what she did.

What she did not know is that this refugee boy was not interested in Susanna. He was only leading her on, in order for his older brother to get to her.

One night, she went over to see her refugee crush, only to be kept in a room by his older brother. The brother Ali raped her that night. According to witnesses, Ali later bragged about raping her all night long.

At the end of it all, little Susanna was dead. Her phone, shoes, and valuables were stolen. To make matters worse, Ali messaged Susanna's mom on WhatsApp, pretending to be her and giving some excuse that she was going to be away a few more days. Eventually Susanna was reported missing.

Her mom went searching for her with Ali's brother. She spoke to Ali's mother. They denied knowing anything. The crime is typical of the Muslim community. Everyone is involved - nobody talks. The target is a non-Muslim 'slut' that is groomed and treated like trash.

The killer, Ali Bashar, is simultaneously under investigation of a previous rape of an eleven-year-old girl. According to a witness, he 'has a thing for virgins'.

The Green party, who claimed it went against protocol, halted a minute of silence for Susanna's death in the Bundestag. Moreover, they claimed the mother should not let herself be used by the 'far-right' to politicize her daughter's death.

Susanna's mother, however, claimed she did not mind the attention and wished that it would change Merkel's policy. She is afraid for her other daughter. However, childless Merkel, so she says, cannot understand her pain.

German Gangs

With regards to gangs, Germany already has a criminal underworld dominated by Arab families. Now the arrival of so many more Arabs has led to one group of Arabs trying to take over control from another group of Arabs. German organized crime, as in, by actual Germans, appears to be missing. [8]

Young Men in Asylum Centers

The German government claims that the overrepresentation in crime in the migrant groups is partially due to migrants being for the majority young men, a group that is always relatively more criminal than other groups, regardless of nationality.

Despite that claim being true, it does not challenge the claim that such immigrant men are still more likely to engage in criminal activity than their German native counterparts when corrected for the same age categories.

Moreover, the government article continues to show that most crimes committed by asylum seekers are committed against other asylum seekers - likely due to the fact that they are living in the same temporary housing. I am not sure if they intend this to somehow cool down the concern about migrant criminality. Doesn't it just mean that even groups of refugees cannot live together peacefully? Shouldn't they feel united and glad to have reached safety, instead of continuing the violence they supposedly flee?

It does not seem to support the idea that migrants are supposed to flee violence and seek peace and a new life. Yes, circumstances in an asylum center are likely not pleasant, but is that an excuse to engage in physical violence?

Moreover, the German government article actually confirms that some nationalities are indeed overrepresented in crime statistics, even when comparing the asylum seekers between themselves. What does that mean? What are the consequences? [10] "Aus den Maghreb-Staaten Algerien, Marokko und Tunesien kamen 11 % aller tatverdächtigen Zuwanderer, obwohl sie nur 2,4 % der Asylsuchenden stellten." The quote above is translated as, "Out of the suspects 11% came from the Maghreb (Algeria, Morocco, Tunisia), despite being only 2.4% of the group of asylum seekers."

So despite claiming that the difference in crime is not cultural, but instead purely due to the fact that most migrants are young men, they do admit there are significant differences in criminal behavior between countries of origin. They admit it, but they ignore it. They have no explanation (culture, attitude?) of where such differences may come from.

Moreover, they claim that life in an asylum center itself is likely a cause of increased violence. That still doesn't really make sense when you think about it. If you are fleeing war and persecution, and you finally reach your safe haven, shouldn't you be happy and relieved? Even when you are stressed about whether or not you'll be accepted, shouldn't you be smart enough to recognize that beating up another person is likely not going to help your cause? And if these people are so lightly inflammable, doesn't that prove the point that they are not to be desired?

I have not seen any comparable evidence of Jewish prisoners in concentration camps, or prisoners of war held in POW-camps, or any other comparable situation, where living together in close quarters was used as an excuse for increased violence.

It becomes even stranger when you admit that the differences in criminality do not stop when they leave the asylum center. Even for second-generation Moroccans, the difference in criminal behavior persists.

Then, of course, the excuse is given that it is purely due to socio-economic factors. So time and time again, the same trick is used. Whenever it is observed that migrants do commit more crime, excuses are made that are to explain away the entirety of the difference. In addition, those excuses are only made when first of all statistics are kept to even be able to prove the difference. Out of fear for 'discrimination', many countries purposefully do not track it.

"Muslims know that Islam clashes with Western Civilization. They make no bones about choosing Islam over their new home country, like the Syrians in Germany, or the Somali at Ohio State University. They are very open and honest on polls, because they know they have nothing to fear from the governments that welcomed them with open arms."
- *Milo Yiannopoulos*

Notes:

[1]   https://www.snopes.com/fact-check/refugee-invaders-meme/

[2]   https://www.bbc.com/news/world-europe-45419466

[3] https://www.infomigrants.net/en/post/18506/murder-of-young-boy-in-frankfurt-prompts-debate-on-immigrant-crime-statistics

[4]   https://rmx.news/article/article/germany-proportion-of-crimes-committed-by-migrants-surges-according-to-police-data

[5]   https://www.badische-zeitung.de/freiburg/fall-maria-l-polizei-freiburg-verhaftet-tatverdaechtigen-wohl-in-strassenbahn--130613711.html

[6] https://www.nytimes.com/2018/01/17/world/europe/germany-teen-murder-migrant.html?_r=0

[7]   https://www.jpost.com/Magazine/Murder-in-Mainz-574162

[8]   https://www.dw.com/en/new-migrants-put-germanys-established-crime-gangs-under-pressure/a-51408164

[9]   https://eufactcheck.eu/factcheck/mostly-false-crime-in-germany-is-up-10-plus-since-migrants-were-accepted%EF%BB%BF/

[10] https://www.integrationsbeauftragte.de/ib-de/service/daten-und-fakten/sind-fluechtlinge-krimineller-als-der-rest-der-bevoelkerung--354618

[11] https://www.independent.co.uk/news/world/europe/cologne-new-year-s-eve-mass-sex-attacks-leaked-document-a7130476.html

[12] https://thecorrespondent.com/4401/time-for-the-facts-what-do-we-know-about-cologne-four-months-later/1073698080444-e20ada1b

NUMBERS IN THE NETHERLANDS

"We want to make our own Netherlands, to close our borders and to keep all that money that we give to the foreigners, there is billions, to Africa for development, to Brussels, to Greece, to asylum seekers in the Netherlands, we will stop that and give all that money to the Dutch people living in the Netherlands."

- Geert Wilders

The Netherlands is known for its prostitutes and easily accessible weed. It has managed to avoid suffering from terror attacks, despite all countries surrounding it not being able to say the same. One curious thing about the Dutch is that they tend to have a good amount of statistics; including statistics on migrant crime that most other countries tend to hide or complicate.

The Statistics

The head economist of the Central Bureau of Statistics, Peter Hein van Mulligen, published a tweet early in 2021 claiming that migrant men are becoming less criminal. He used statistics to prove it, and yes, he was right.

What he failed to include in his optimistic tweet, however, was that migrant men were still far more likely to engage in criminal behavior than their Dutch counterparts. Peter Hein used the fact that non-Western migrants were growing as a group in the Netherlands, while simultaneously crime rates were dropping, to 'prove' his implicit point that the arrival of migrants was making the country safer.

That conclusion was completely ignorant towards the underlying data. Now the data used is the amount of suspects of a crime per 10.000 inhabitants, split into different groups. In 2010 for Dutch natives between 18 and 25, 329 out of 10.000 had been suspected of a crime. For non-Western immigrants in the same age category that number was 832 out of 10.000. That is 2.5 times as many as their Dutch counterparts.

By 2019, numbers for both had dropped. For Dutch men, of the same age category, in 2019, 150 out of 10.000 had been suspected of a crime. For non-Western immigrants that number was 428. That is 2.8 times as many as their Dutch counterparts.

So yes, overall crime suspects dropped, but non-Western immigrants are still far more likely to engage in criminal behavior than their Dutch counterparts, even more so than in 2010. The total number of people suspected of a crime nearly halved in the period between 2010 and 2019 as well.

Since this tracks total suspects of crimes, crimes where no suspect is found are excluded. It is worth noting as well that there are no reports of discrimination having a significant influence on these metrics, a similar overrepresentation of non-Western immigrants is seen when it comes to convictions. [1]

The decrease in crime committed by non-Western immigrants does not show successful integration or assimilation of the immigrants. Instead, it shows an overall, general downward trend in criminality. This is partially explained due to the police not handling all cases, and many Dutch will not even bother to report their stolen bicycle to the police for example. It is also due to more cameras, and more available evidence such as fingerprints and DNA.

On top of that, it has gotten far more difficult to steal cars for example. Houses have more and better locks. Moreover, heroin junks, a group that used to commit a lot of the crime in the 1980's, have all but disappeared.

The point has to be repeated that despite this general downward trend, non-Western immigrants are even more overrepresented in crime statistics than they were before.

Nor do we see a sharp drop between first and second-generation immigrants from these areas. Although second generation immigrants from European countries are on almost the same level of criminality as the Dutch, second-generation non-Western immigrants remain far higher. If there is a decline, it is small, and sometimes there is an increase instead. Between the groups of migrants, Moroccans are near the top, preceded by immigrants from the Dutch colonies in the Caribbean. The Turkish sit in the middle, with Iraqis and Afghans grouped together as 'others' closer to the bottom - though still far above the Dutch. [3]

4.6a Schuldigverklaringen rechter in eerste aanleg

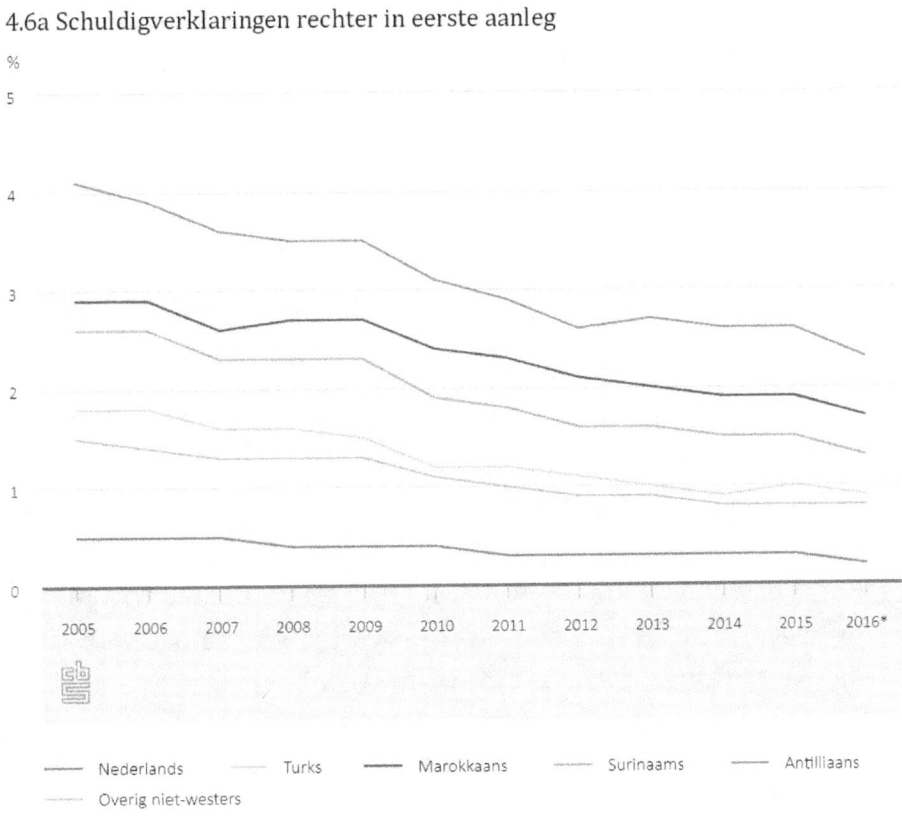

4.6a Declared guilty %

Nederlands = Dutch, Turks = Turkish, Marokkaans = Moroccan, Surinaams = Suriname, Antilliaans = Dutch Caribbean, Over niet-westers = Other non-Western

Source: CBS (Centraal Bureau voor de Statistiek)

Asylum Seekers

In 2018 there was an increase in the amount of crime where the perpetrator was an asylum seeker. This was odd, since the amount of asylum seekers in the country had actually decreased. The initial excuse applied was that most of the new asylum seekers came from safe countries such as Morocco and Algeria, which meant they had a poor chance of getting their asylum request approved.

Though, at the same time, despite the difficulty at getting approved, it would be nearly impossible to return them to their home countries due to a lack of cooperation. Approved or not, these migrants were here to stay, and they knew that. Of course they knew, it's why they bothered to come in the first place.

Nevertheless, how does having poor chances of getting approved lead to increased crime? Surely engaging in crime will not help your already feeble position. Once more, a coincidental correlation is used as a supposed causal relationship.

It ignores the fact that Moroccans and Algerians that are already legal citizens in the Netherlands are also overrepresented when it comes to crime. But for that group a different excuse is found. Moreover, not only crimes such as theft had increased, but also sexual crimes and rapes. How can an increase in sexual crimes be explained by having poor chances of having your asylum request approved? What possible thought process can justify that? [2]

Moroccans

In every country, North-Africans seem to pop up as bringers of the highest levels of criminality. Moroccans, Algerians, Tunisians. Of course, their behavior is explained by their socio-economic status, the supposed racism they suffer, and the whole list of other excuses. But what if part of the problem simply sits with them? What if it is culture that plays an important role?

These countries used to form the Barbary States, an Ottoman protectorate that roamed the Mediterranean, taking Europeans as slaves wherever they could. Europe does not need to have a sensation of guilt towards these peoples; they were never taken as slaves.

As far as racism goes, the Turkish inhabitants of Amsterdam are actually most negative about their Moroccan counterparts. Being an immigrant group themselves, they can speak more candidly.

Besides, shouldn't racism apply to all groups of non-white immigrants equally? Then why do some manage to do relatively well, while others stand out in such a negative way? [4]

Is it really so unfair to ask the Moroccan community as to why they are so overrepresented in crime? Is it racist to request that they look inward and attempt to change their behavior?

It is hardly surprising that the Dutch drug trade is controlled by groups of Moroccans, often coined the 'Mocro Mafia'. Mocro is simply slang for Moroccan. The public face of drug consumption in the Netherlands is that of public coffee shops, but a far greater drug world exists in people using WhatsApp to reach their local drug dealer, often a Moroccan youth, who will drop by on his scooter. [5] The Mocro Mafia is so infamous that it has been translated to a TV series which has aired three seasons so far. The police fail to get a grip on this type of crime. Since there are no victims, there are no suspects, and no crime statistics.

Nevertheless, the Mocro Mafia is active throughout Europe. Some time ago, a Moroccan with a Dutch passport was arrested for trying to smuggle thousands of kilos of cocaine into Europe. He moved the goods through Romania, using the port in Constanta, and was arrested at an airport in Spain. [7]

Another type of crime where the Moroccans dominate is in the role of 'loverboy'. It is a pretty name for what is essentially the grooming of young girls into a life of prostitution. By sweet-talking, gift giving, and macho acting, they make young girls fall in love with them. Then, when they have isolated the girl, they force the girl to have sex with other men. Sometimes they get the girls drug-addicted to ensure they are fully dependent.

Such grooming is only one option. In other cases, the girls are basically kidnapped and held as captives. The practice is similar to the Ottomans and Barbary pirates raiding small fishing villages and taking all women captive. The women were sent to Constantinople, to serve as sex slaves, or 'concubines' in the Sultan's harem. Because yes, those harems were generally made up of European, white, slave girls. This century-old tradition appears to continue. Moroccans push girls into a life of prostitution, where other foreign man, including Turks, can pay a small fee in exchange for sex with them.

Every year more than a thousand underage Dutch girls are groomed and forced into prostitution. To do away with fancy terms such as loverboy and prostitute, these are young girls forced into the life of a sex-slave while their criminal masters rake in the money. The gangs will tell the girls they can serve fewer customers that day, as long as they assist in getting some of their friends 'groomed' as well. Other stories tell us that the gangsters will roll a dice; the number of eyes will be how many men the girl has to have sex with that day. It's a huge, though mostly invisible underground network. [6]

More Statistics

The data on the right all concerns suspects per 10.000 inhabitants, diversified for native Dutch, European migrants, non-Western migrants, Moroccan background, Dutch Carribean background, Surinamese background, Turkish background, or other non-Western background. This applies to total groups, not split for age categories. Since non-Western migrants tend to be younger, and young people commit more crime, this puts them on a slight disadvantage, but not significantly. Moreover, we wish to show the effect these groups of migrants have on crime in the Netherlands, that part of it can be explained by them being younger is somewhat irrelevant, as crime is nevertheless committed.

Onderwerp ▼		Totaal	Nederlandse achtergrond	Westerse migratieachtergrond	Niet-westerse migratieachtergrond	Marokko	(voormalige) Ned. Antillen,Aruba	Suriname	Turkije	Overige niet-westerse migratieachterg...
Geregistreerde verdachten										
Verdachten per 10 000 inwoners										
Totaal verdachten van misdrijven	aantal	90	65	95	238	349	406	268	191	174
Verdachten van vermogensmisdrijven										
Totaal vermogensmisdrijven	aantal	31	20	34	91	141	173	100	52	71
Diefstal/verduistering en inbraak	aantal	24	16	28	69	105	138	78	35	55
Diefstal van fiets	aantal	1	1	1	3	5	8	3	2	3
Diefstal van bromfiets/snorfiets	aantal	1	0	1	3	5	6	3	2	2
Diefstal van personenauto	aantal	0	0	0	1	2	2	2	0	1
Diefstal uit/vanaf personenauto	aantal	1	0	1	2	8	2	2	1	1
Straatroof	aantal	1	0	1	5	7	12	7	2	3
Zakkenrollerij	aantal	0	0	0	1	1	1	0	0	1
Winkeldiefstal	aantal	14	9	18	35	40	81	43	13	32
Diefstal/inbraak uit woning	aantal	1	1	1	6	14	8	5	3	3
Diefstal/inbraak uit schuur/garage	aantal	0	0	0	1	1	1	1	1	0
Verdachten vernieling en openbare orde										
Totaal vernieling en openbare orde	aantal	14	10	12	36	56	58	39	26	27
Vernieling en beschadiging	aantal	6	5	6	15	22	25	17	10	11
Vernieling aan auto	aantal	2	1	2	4	5	6	4	4	3
Openbare orde misdrijven	aantal	5	4	5	15	22	22	16	12	12
Openlijke geweldpleging	aantal	3	2	3	10	16	14	8	10	7
Brandstichting	aantal	1	1	1	1	2	2	1	1	1
Verdachten van geweldsmisdrijven										
Totaal geweldsmisdrijven	aantal	24	16	21	70	95	125	77	60	52
Mishandeling	aantal	15	11	14	43	57	77	47	36	33
Bedreiging en stalking	aantal	7	5	6	23	35	42	26	21	15
Seksueel misdrijf	aantal	1	1	1	4	4	6	4	3	4
Verdachten van verkeersmisdrijven										
Totaal verkeersmisdrijven	aantal	23	18	26	49	70	78	62	49	31
Verlaten plaats ongeval	aantal	3	2	3	8	15	6	7	8	5
Rijden onder invloed	aantal	17	14	20	33	40	60	46	31	21
Verdachten van drugsmisdrijven	aantal	9	6	10	27	52	41	26	25	16
Verdachten van vuurwapenmisdrijven	aantal	4	3	4	12	15	29	14	11	7

Bron: CBS

We can see that for the Dutch only 65 out of 10.000 become a suspect, while for non-Western migrants this number sits at 238. Nearly four times as high. There is not a single sub-category where the native Dutch are more likely to be suspected of a crime, than the immigrant population.

When it comes to sexual misconduct, including rape, non-Western immigrants are four times more likely to be suspects. Migrants from the Dutch Caribbean are six times more likely to be a suspect. When it comes to other types of violent crime, the Dutch Caribbean migrants, coming from the old Dutch colonies, are around eight times as likely to be suspected of a crime. That is a massive difference!

Western, European, migrants are no more likely than the native Dutch to commit such crimes. Another indicator that rape has to do with culture and origin, not socio-economic status. European migrants do score higher on all other sub-categories than the Dutch, but the differences are relatively minor, especially when compared to the non-Western groups.

Moreover, the European migrants only score notably higher in categories of theft, which is somewhat unsurprising considering this category includes the infamous Eastern European gangs and the equally infamous Sinti population.

Still non-Western migrants score three times higher than European migrants do in theft also. In addition, even the 'least criminal' category of non-Western migrants scores more than twice as high as the

European migrants. So yes, Turks are less criminal than Moroccans are, but they are still far more criminal than both the Dutch as well as the European migrants.

When it comes to drug-related crime, Moroccans are almost nine times more likely than the Dutch to be suspects. Further proof of the Moroccans controlling the drug trade in the Netherlands.

Even with regards to DUIs (Driving Under Influence) the Islamic Moroccans and Turks are twice as prevalent as the native Dutch, and more prevalent than the European migrants which includes the notoriously stereotypical drunk Polish migrants. If we were to assume they are pious Muslims, we would expect to see fewer Moroccans and Turks receive fines for DUIs. Do they actually drink more alcohol, or do they simply care less about the law and are more likely to drive after drinking? [8]

MIGRANT CRIME IN EUROPE

Onderwerp ▼		Totaal	Nederlandse achtergrond	Westerse migratieachtergrond	Niet-westerse migratieachtergrond	Marokko	(voormalige) Ned. Antillen, Aruba	Suriname	Turkije	Overige niet-westerse migratieachterg...
		25 tot 45 jaar Mannen	25 tot 45 jaar Mannen	25 tot 45 jaar Mannen	25 tot 45 jaar Mannen	25 tot 45 jaar Mannen	25 tot 45 jaar Mannen	25 tot 45 jaar Mannen	25 tot 45 jaar Mannen	25 tot 45 jaar Mannen
Geregistreerde verdachten										
Verdachten per 10 000 inwoners										
Totaalverdachten van misdrijven	aantal	210	148	206	443	723	734	582	395	280
Verdachten van vermogensmisdrijven										
Totaal vermogensmisdrijven	aantal	53	36	56	117	216	201	132	82	81
Diefstal/verduistering en inbraak	aantal	40	28	43	84	156	158	97	51	59
Diefstal van fiets	aantal	3	3	2	6	12	12	5	5	4
Diefstal van bromfiets/snorfiets	aantal	1	1	0	1	11	4	1	4	1
Diefstal van personenauto	aantal	1	1	1	2	2	1	1	1	1
Diefstal uit/vanaf personenauto	aantal	2	2	2	4	4	3	3	1	1
Straatroof	aantal	1	1	0	3	15	7	4	3	1
Zakkenrollerij	aantal	0	0	0	1	6	4	4	1	1
Winkeldiefstal	aantal	18	12	24	34	43	75	38	38	33
Diefstal/inbraak uit bedrijf/kantoor	aantal	0	0	0	1	2	.	.	1	1
Overige diefstal/verduistering/inbraak	aantal	1	1	3	9	28	11	1	5	4
Diefstal/inbraak uit woning	aantal	4	3	3	9	13	13	12	5	5
Diefstal/inbraak uit schuur/garage	aantal	1	1	0	1	2	2	1	1	1
Verdachten vernieling en openbare orde										
Totaal vernieling en openbare orde	aantal	31	23	26	65	111	103	88	50	44
Vernieling en beschadiging	aantal	17	14	14	34	58	56	48	25	22
Vernieling aan auto	aantal	5	4	4	9	13	13	13	10	5
Openbare orde misdrijven	aantal	9	7	8	20	27	26	26	16	16
Openlijke geweldpleging	aantal	4	3	4	8	12	11	9	11	5
Brandstichting	aantal	1	1	1	2	5	2	2	2	2
Verdachten van Geweldsmisdrijven										
Totaal geweldsmisdrijven	aantal	65	42	52	156	233	282	200	158	104
Mishandeling	aantal	41	27	35	96	137	186	127	84	64
Bedreiging en stalking	aantal	22	14	16	55	94	94	71	50	33
Seksueel misdrijf	aantal	4	3	3	8	9	12	10	5	8
Verdachten van verkeersmisdrijven										
Totaal verkeersmisdrijven	aantal	69	53	75	124	186	215	194	120	69
Verlaten plaats ongeval	aantal	6	4	7	13	27	11	14	12	8
Rijden onder invloed	aantal	53	42	60	88	119	173	148	82	49
Verdachten van drugsmisdrijven	aantal	26	17	24	61	129	93	72	56	31
Verdachten van vuurwapenmisdrijven	aantal	9	6	8	18	26	54	24	19	9

Bron: CBS

Dutch Caribbean

Filtering for age categories doesn't make it look any better. When filtered for the age category of 25 to 45, an age during which people ought to behave properly, and can no longer claim any youthful ignorance, non-Western migrants continue to be strongly overrepresented.

Especially Moroccans and Dutch Caribbean migrants jump out, being suspected of a crime five times as often as Dutch natives are. In the violent crime category, migrants from the Dutch Caribbean are still seven times more criminal than their Dutch counterparts - after adjusting for age.

This is what I meant when I said that filtering for age does not have a significant impact. Non-Western migrants are still overrepresented in every single category, by various multiples. For violent crime of the Caribbean migrants, the multiple dropped from eight to seven after adjusting for age category. A drop for sure, but nowhere near the native Dutch population.

To help you imagine the severity of such a multiple, imagine two villages of 10.000 people each. One is Dutch, the other Caribbean. Where one suffers 42 cases of violent crime, the other suffers 282 such cases. In the Dutch village theft takes place 36 times, in the Caribbean village theft takes place 201 times. Can such differences really be attributed to being a victim of racism? Can it be attributed to purely socio-economic factors? A 7% increase perhaps, but a 700% increase?

Not surprisingly, crime rates are high in the Dutch Caribbean as well. So much so that Dutch tourists are given reassurance not to worry too much, and still come to the islands. Now the explanations are not racism or socio-economic position, but the vicinity of the South-American world of drugs. Since drugs do not explain non-drug related violence, a secondary reason is given; fatherless homes and youth unemployment.

Is it a coincidence that such negative factors are simply replaced by racism and socio-economic status when they reach the Netherlands? Or could we perhaps conclude that they bring their criminal behavior over with them? Besides, there is no way to measure the actual 'amount' of racism such migrants suffer, if they suffer any at all. Most live in the big cities, where the native Dutch form an absolute minority, and the majority is formed by various groups of migrants.

There is no measurement either to compare Dutch natives from a low socio-economic background to migrants from a similar socio-economic background, meaning the claim that it is caused by socio-economic background is completely baseless and nothing more than a purely hypothetical theory.

Christopher Hitchens, talking about the existence of God, stated "What can be asserted without evidence can also be dismissed without evidence." Now we are not talking about God, but it appears Hitchens' Razor can be applied nonetheless. If a hypothesis, such as socioeconomics being the cause and not ethnicity, is presented without evidence, then it can be rejected without evidence.

I find myself sometimes in a discussion where the other person urges me to present evidence disproving their baseless hypothesis. Yet why am I forced to prove their hypothesis wrong, when they have given no reason why their hypothesis would be right to begin with? I see no logical reason why socioeconomics should bring about more violence and sexual assault. More theft? Sure. That makes sense. So I am presented with an illogical hypothesis, for which there is no supporting evidence, and I am expected to prove that this hypothesis is wrong. Of course socioeconomics does influence crime, many things do. Ethnicity, religion, or culture, is not the only driving force. The hypothesis that this book presents, however, is that origin, or the presence of a non-Western migrant background, for whatever underlying reason there may be, does indeed impact crime. And that that is something that we ought to acknowledge and take into account.

Both theories, racism and socio-economics, lack any sort of data to back up its claims. Meanwhile, similar trends of violence in the countries of origin match the above-average level of violence they exhibit in Dutch society. A very clear indicator that criminality sits with the individual, rather than with the environment.

"Moroccan boys never steal from Moroccans."

- Pim Fortuyn

Notes:

[1]   https://waarheidsdemocratie.nl/fact-check-cbs-hoofdeconoom-meer-migratie-minder-misdaad/

[2]   https://www.ad.nl/politiek/meer-misdrijven-migranten-vooral-door-algerijnen-en-marokkanen~a9a0225f/?referrer=https%3A%2F%2Fwww.google.com%2F#:~:text=zetten%20%C2%A9%20ANP-,Meer%20misdrijven%20migranten%2C%20vooral%20door%20Algerijnen%20en%20Marokkanen,seksuele%20misdrijven%20en%20twee%20moorden

[3]   https://longreads.cbs.nl/integratie-2018/criminaliteit/

[4]   https://www.trouw.nl/nieuws/de-etnisch-culturele-kant-van-criminaliteit-verzwijgen-we-liever~b6c88152/?referrer=https%3A%2F%2Fwww.google.com%2F

[5] https://www.binnenlandsbestuur.nl/Uploads/2019/8/onderzoeksrapport-de-achterkant-van-amsterdam.pdf

[6] http://www.clovisinstitute.org/loverboy/

[7]   https://www.bd.nl/brabant/hoe-undercoveragenten-een-nederlandse-drugsbaron-in-de-val-lokten~ab94adf2/?referrer=https%3A%2F%2Fwww.google.com%2F

[8]
https://opendata.cbs.nl/statline/#/CBS/nl/dataset/
81947NED/table?dl=4D117

UNREST IN THE UNITED KINGDOM

"Heaven take thy soul, and England keep my bones!"

– William Shakespeare

The United Kingdom once ruled the world, but for the last decades, the process has been reversing. Countless migrants from former colonies have moved to England.

The largest groups in England have been migrants from India and Pakistan, with numerous Africans joining as well. What has been the effect on crime in the UK?

It must be said here that data is complicated by the UK mostly diversifying between 'foreign-born' and 'native', though due to England's policy of relatively open borders going back decades, many of the Pakistani are, for example, already second-generation. A group completely excluded.

In other cases, it becomes even more difficult as they differentiate only 'foreign nationals', meaning anyone that has obtained a UK passport by now is no longer split from the native population.

Nor does the data tend to differentiate between European and non-European migrants, though for example in the data from the Netherlands we see a huge gap in criminal behavior between those groups.

More Migrants Equals More Crime

On The Conversation [2] we read, "Immigrant populations tend to be very concentrated, with people tending to reside in areas with existing communities. My recent research shows that throughout England and Wales, areas where immigrants from one single background make up a significant majority of the immigrant population, tend to be low in crime. Nearly as low in crime as the areas with small immigrant populations."

This is an interesting conclusion, so I looked into the actual paper that was written. In effect, it showed that more migrants brought more crime, showing an upward correlation. The conclusion is based on the fact that as the group of immigrants from the same area of the world continued to grow, at some point this positive trend reversed and crime dropped slightly again. This happened fairly quickly for areas with European migrants, a bit later for areas with African migrants, though interestingly, this drop never took place for areas with more and more Asian immigrants. For that category, crime just continued to increase. [1]

Crime Statistics on Race

Despite not tracking the proper migration background, we were able to find data that separated groups based on race. The main categories are white, black, Asian (meaning India, Pakistan, and Bangladesh), and other. [3]

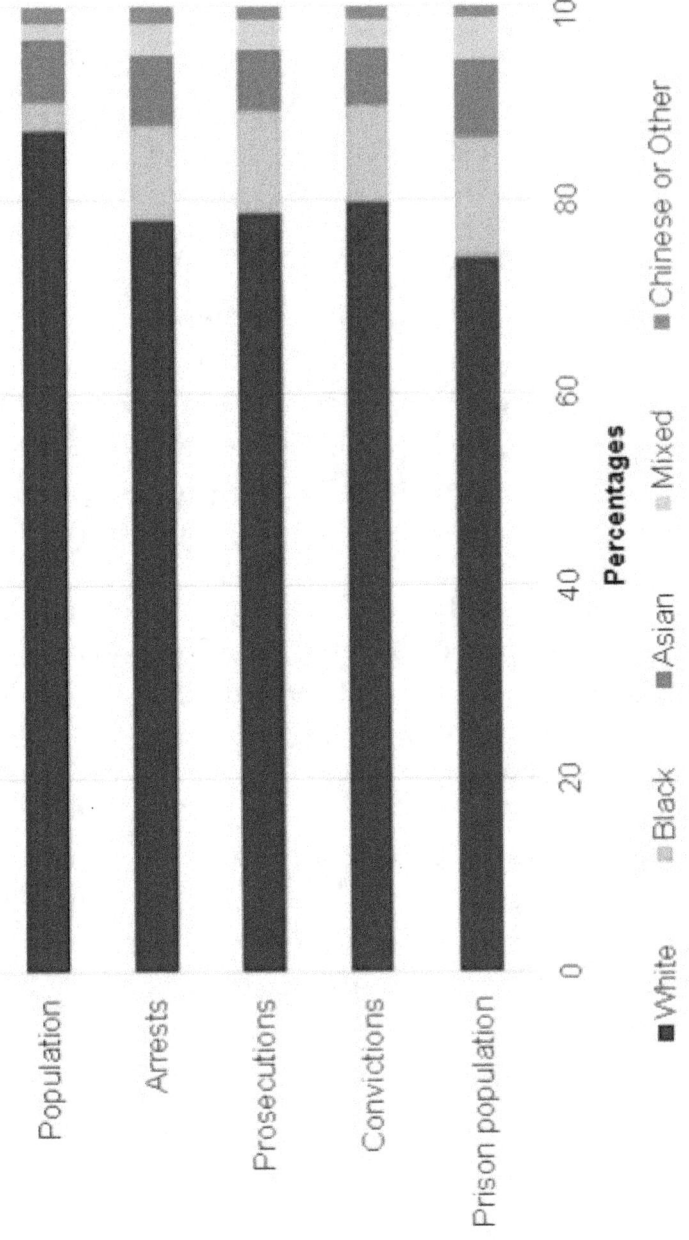

Figure 1.01: Ethnicity proportions throughout the CJS, 2016[1]

We immediately see the overrepresentation of black people in all categories, from arrests to persecutions, to convictions to prison population. Their even greater overrepresentation in the prison population may indicate that black people are convicted for more severe crimes and serve longer sentences.

The other group that shows clear overrepresentation are those that are mixed-race, a group that mostly consists of white-black or white-Asian. The Asian group only appears to be overrepresented in the prison population, with a slight underrepresentation when it comes to convictions. Asian data is complicated to interpret, since the Muslim Pakistani are combined with the non-Muslim Indians.

A black person is about four times as likely to be in prison, compared to a white person. Do note here that the 'white' population includes immigrants as well. This is not merely 'white British' so it includes the immigrants from Europe.

Black and Mixed jump out in a negative way for every single step along the way. The group of Asians shows some increases in arrests, while the white and Chinese or other group are equally low.

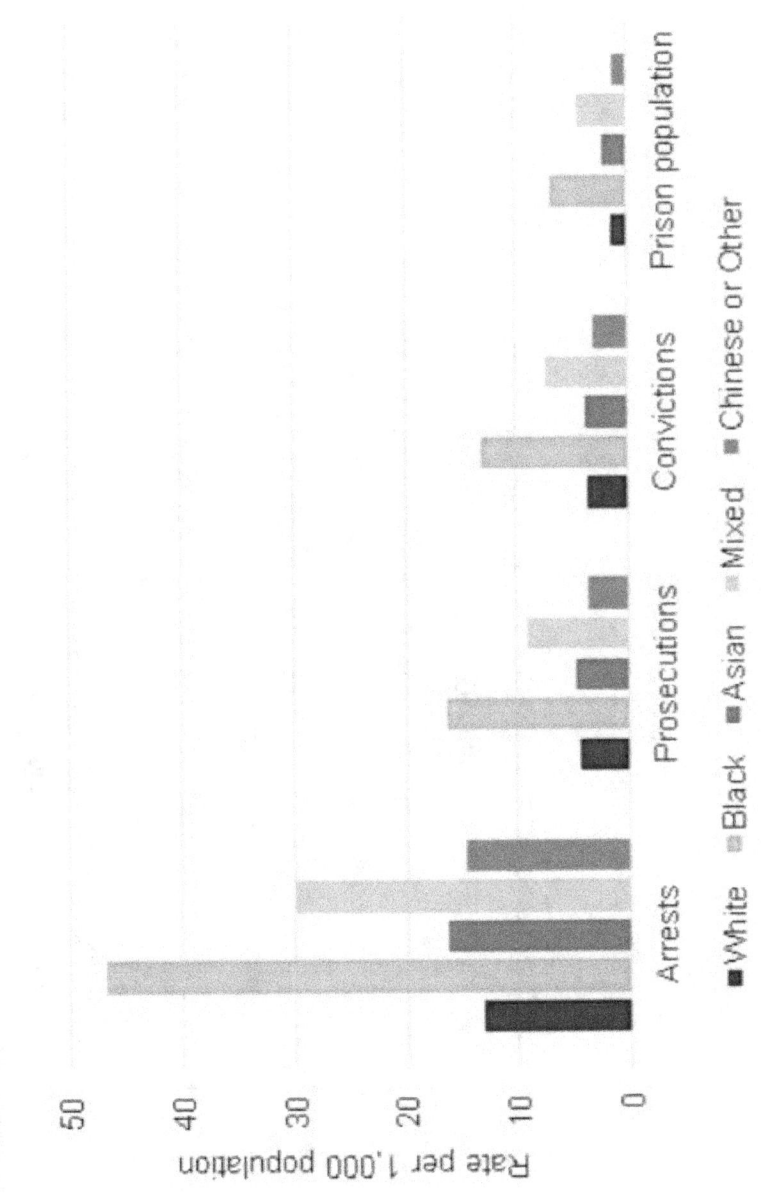

Figure 1.01: Rates per 1,000 population throughout the CJS, by ethnicity, England and Wales 2016[3]

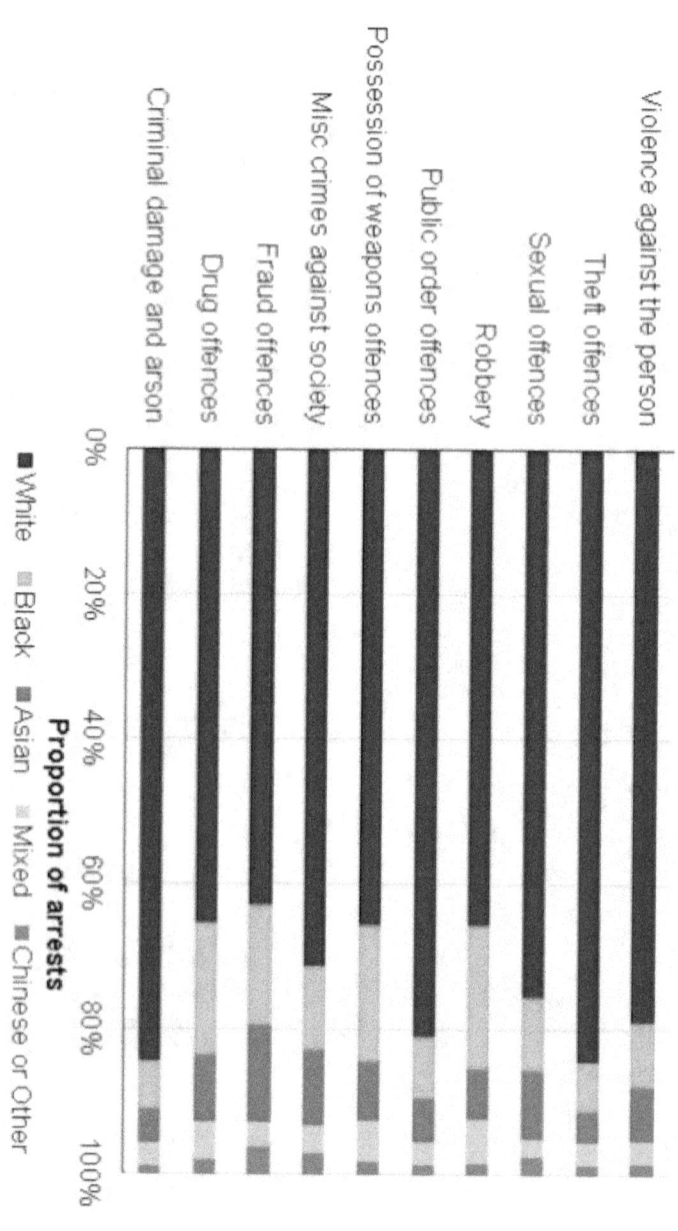

Figure 4.09: Proportion of arrests within each offence group, by ethnicity, 2016/17 (Source: Table 4.20)

As we would expect based on the Dutch data, whites score higher (better said, they score a 'normal' score) when it comes to theft, which can be at part explained due to European migrants as the Dutch data showed. Not to deny that the white British aren't capable of crime themselves.

Still, this higher score only sets them at the level that would be expected if all groups committed crime equal to their proportion of the population. The same applies for the section involving arson.

In sexual offences and fraud we see the largest overrepresentations of the Asian group. While blacks are overrepresented in nearly every category, most notably in the possession of weapons, robbery, and drug offences. Although drug offences are for a large part the possession of drugs, which some consider a victimless crime; it is important to note that the overrepresentation persists excluding drug possession as well.

Again in the next graph, we see a rate for blacks being arrested more than three times as high as for whites. The mixed group sits neatly in the middle between the white and black averages. This is what one would expect when the root cause is related to their migrant background and ethnicity.

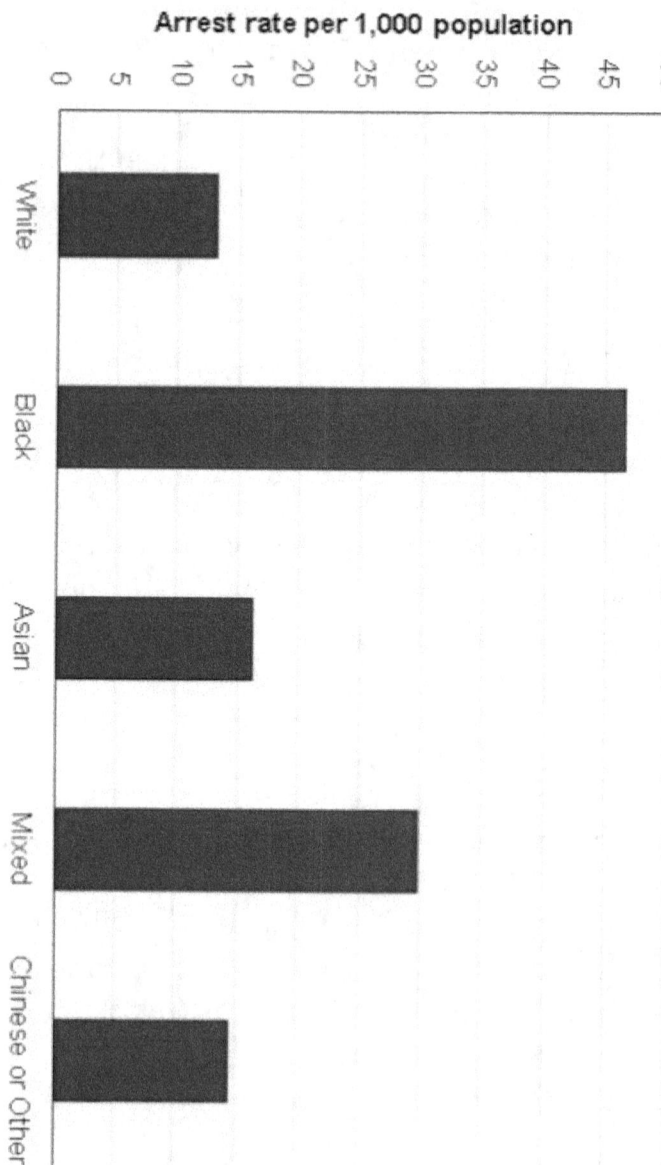

Figure 4.12: Arrest rate per 1,000 members of the population (aged 10 and over) by self-identified ethnicity, 2016/17 (Source: Table 4.23)

Table II.02: Concordance between ethnicity figures for White, Black and Asian: 2010 to 2014, MoJ Court Proceedings Database

	Ethnic appearance (4+1 classification) (percentages)					
	White	Black	Asian	Other	Not stated	Total (all)
White	98%	0%	0%	0%	1%	100%
Black	1%	96%	1%	1%	1%	100%
Asian	2%	1%	90%	6%	1%	100%
Mixed	17%	64%	10%	4%	5%	100%
Chinese or Other	36%	8%	12%	38%	6%	100%
Not stated	17%	4%	1%	1%	76%	100%
Total (all)	72%	10%	5%	1%	12%	100%

Self-identified ethnicity (5+1 ethnicity classification) (percentages)

Source: Court Proceedings database

That the mixed group sits in between white and black makes sense when we can see that a majority of those that self-identify as 'mixed' have a black ethnic appearance according to the government data presented above.

When it comes to mental health, the biggest factors we see is that whites are far more likely to be diagnosed with depression, while every other group is far more likely to be diagnosed with schizophrenia. Blacks are four times as likely to be diagnosed with schizophrenia compared to whites, but even the Chinese and other are more than twice as likely.

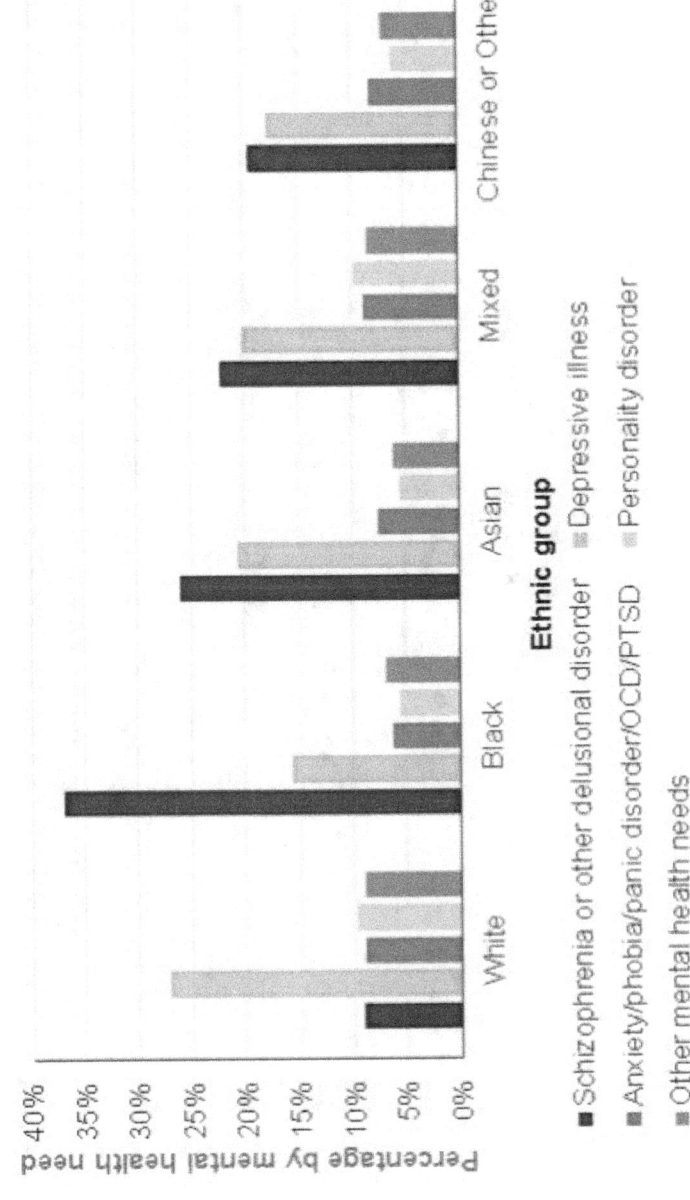

Figure 4.17: Offenders using national Liaison and Diversion services by mental health need and ethnicity (percentages), 2016/17 (Source: Table 4.32c)

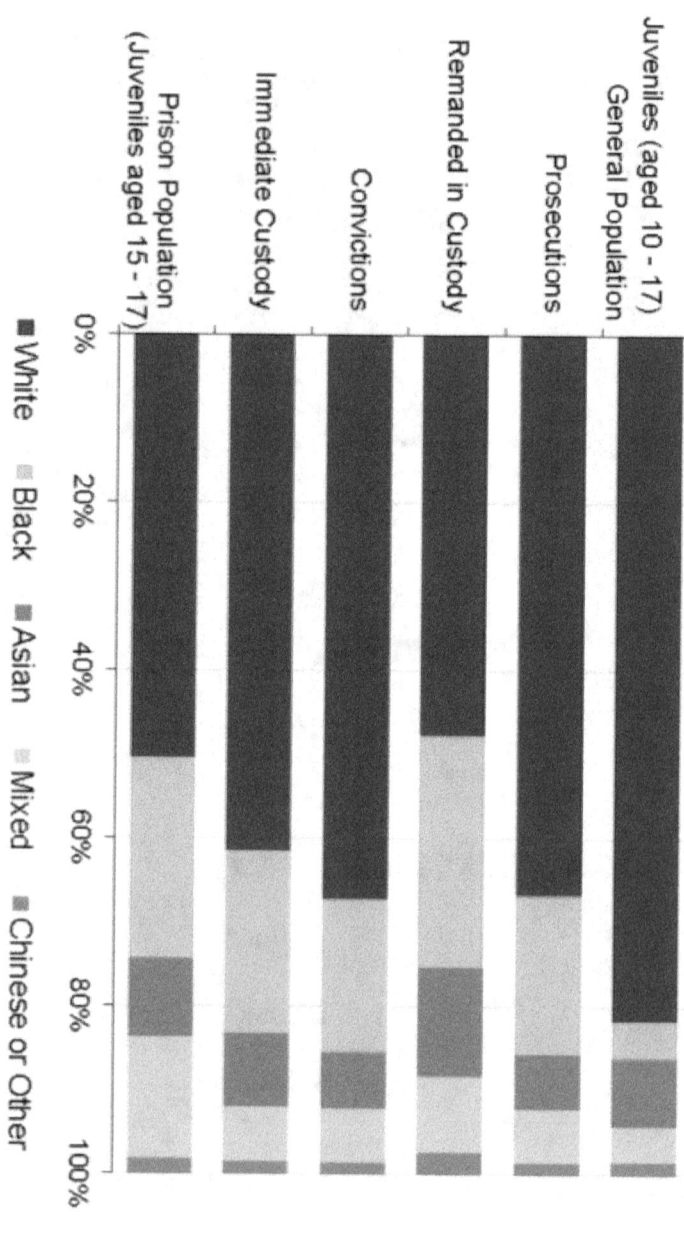

Figure 6.03: Youth Summary Chart to show proportion of young people in the criminal justice system, broken down by ethnicity, 2016, England and Wales

When we only look at juveniles, in order to ensure that the increased black crime is not due to a higher proportion of juveniles in that ethnic category, we see that the overrepresentation continues and is actually even stronger when looking only at those aged 15 to 17. Despite being more than 80% of the juvenile population, whites make up only 50% of the juvenile prison population.

The data above somehow fails to show the impact that Asian grooming gangs have on society.

Asian Grooming Gangs

Such grooming gangs are again nothing but a network of pedophile rapists that force young, insecure girls into a life of slavery. Girls are seduced either with compliments and gifts, or, more commonly, with alcohol and drugs. If all else fails, the girls are simply physically taken and locked in a room. It is difficult to comprehend how horrible such crimes really are, as some girls are taken for many years, forced to have sex with thousands of men, with daily beatings and other forms of sadistic torture.

In a recent BBC article it is said, "During a trial lasting more than eight weeks the jury heard the men, who are all of British Pakistani heritage, preyed on the girls' vulnerability before they were sexually assaulted and passed on to other men." [4] The shared Pakistani heritage (sometimes Bangladeshi, formerly East-Pakistan) is a common trend when it comes to these types of crime.

Another article mentions the, "the conviction of 12 men of predominantly British-Pakistani heritage for running a vast child abuse ring in nearby Rochdale in May 2012." [5]

The Pakistani men tend to claim innocence and state that the girls were prostitutes and no coercion had taken place. It is difficult to imagine such a defense being a success, when the girls are underage and even if they consented it would be considered statutory rape.

"Their victims numbered 47 mainly white girls who ringleader Shabir Ahmed, 59, accused of being "prostitutes" and willing sexual participants. He was handed a 19-year sentence." The anti-white racist undertone is hard to deny, "It revealed that at least 1,400 children, most of them white girls aged 11–15, had been sexually abused in Rotherham between 1997 and 2013 by predominantly British-Pakistani men."

Pakistani men as perpetrators, with white British girls as victims. Naz Shah, a member of parliament with Asian ancestry supposedly 'accidentally' retweeted and liked a message saying the Rotherham victims should shut their mouths for the sake of diversity. A very odd accident to occur, to say the least – better phrased, it is an obvious lie. It is nonetheless telling concerning where the loyalties lie for Asian members of parliament. [6]

Such grooming does not only take place in Rotherham or Rochdale, it takes place nationwide. Over 19.000 cases of grooming were identified in 2019, a number that still ignores the decades of grooming that have taken place before. [7]

Despite the crimes having obvious racial characteristics, women are actively attacked for speaking out against the grooming epidemic, exactly because they are accused of promoting racism against the Pakistani community. That these men raped her, is not taken into account. [8]

The nature of the real racism shines through in survivor reports, which all show a clear trend of suffering abuse in the form of "white slut", "white slag", "white cunt", "white bitch", or "fucking gori". Gori being an Asian term for white person. The need to constantly include "white" before every insult, combined with the fact that victims are almost exclusively white, solidifies the racial motive behind these crimes.

It is not uncommon for the girls to get pregnant at the hands of these Pakistani men. Sometimes the children are given up for adoption to a Pakistani family, sometimes the women are punched in the stomach in order for them to miscarry, and sometimes the women end up raising the spawn of their horrible rape with all the love they have left. The English judicial system is nonetheless so messed up, that the rapist father can seek access to the child. [9]

The British have of course sought to deny the fact that these gangs are almost exclusively Asian. Where others participate, it tends to be white women that preferred to lure in other girls, rather than continue to get raped themselves. Still, the BBC claims there is no evidence for such claims, despite high-profile cases such as the ones in Rotherham, Telford, Rochdale, Oxford, Keighley, Peterborough, Newcastle, Aylesbury, Bristol... all consisting of non-white groups of perpetrators.

The Quilliam Foundation published a report confirming that 84% of grooming gangs are Asian, predominantly Pakistani and Muslim. [10] Note; that does not mean that 16% of them are white. That 16% includes African groups, it includes Eastern European mafia, and it includes gypsies. In fact, it showed that fewer than 7% were white. Very odd in a country where whites still form the majority of the inhabitants, plus, let us not forget, that whites formed the vast, near exclusive, majority of the victims.

Not only do they deny the validity of the research which concluded 84% of grooming gangs are Asian, the Guardian also claims that the conclusion as to the motive is completely wrong, saying that it has nothing to do with Muslim culture or misogyny, but that "The issue, he argues, is less about culture or religion than opportunity and circumstance. In many small towns, Asians control the night-time economy – working in takeaways or driving minicabs."

Of course, it is somehow natural for those working in takeaway restaurants to try to groom young girls, because the opportunity presents itself. That is an utterly dire statement to make about the human race as a whole. As if any person represented with opportunity will commit the vilest crimes. As if, given the opportunity, I would want to lock a young girl in my basement and earn money by letting other men rape her. Dear reader, do you? Please feel free to correct me here if I am wrong and this is a natural tendency to have.

The Guardian also states, "Nazir Afzal is the Crown Prosecution Service's former lead on child sexual abuse and the prosecutor most responsible for bringing down grooming gangs. The media, he observes, pounce on cases involving Asians, but often ignore those involving white perpetrators."

Nazir Afzal, a practicing Muslim with Pakistani roots, seeks to defend the role of Muslim Pakistani groups in the grooming gang scandals. Perhaps the media pounces on those cases purely because those cases are the most gruesome. How objective can Nazir be? To give him some credit, he actually tackled some of the grooming gang cases, something his white colleagues were too afraid of, fearing they would appear racist or politically incorrect for pursuing action against criminal Asian gangs.

Of course, his claim that the majority of pedophiles in the United Kingdom are white may be true. It is what would be expected from a majority white country. If 80% of the population is white, under normal circumstances 80% of the pedophiles ought to be white.

It does, however, ignore that there is a difference in the crimes of an individual pedophile that may abuse a single child once, and a group of ten men operating for years, targeting hundreds of girls, and raping a single girl thousands of times.

Although the majority of pedophiles may be white, the majority of victims are white girls who were raped by Asian men. Grooming gangs are almost non-existent in purely white groups.

On Sky News we read that, "Nazir Afzal, who is credited with tackling the issue during his time as Chief Crown Prosecutor in the North West, warned the issue of 'Asian' grooming gangs is being used as a recruitment tool by the far-right."

The question there could be, is it worse that the far-right uses this to recruit people, or is it worse that it is happening in the first place? If there would not be groups of Asian men grooming young white girls, there would not be anything for the far right to recruit with. Do the Green parties abuse climate change to recruit people to their cause?

I am sure someone will review this book saying it is a racist 'pile of crap' exactly for the reason that I discuss such things as Asian grooming gangs. However, I am only reviewing the evidence. I focus on statistics and facts. Are facts racist? If your answer is 'yes', then you need to reassess your worldview. [11]

In case you do not believe the Quilliam Foundation research or that it is biased, there is a second piece of research. "According to the most recent figures, released in 2012 by the National Crime Agency's Child Exploitation and Online Protection Command (CEOP), 100% of child sex offenders in paedophile rings were white. The report says CEOP, an official government body, identifies two types of group-based child sexual exploitation offenders.

Type 1 offenders were those that targeted their victims based on their vulnerability (roughly equivalent of grooming gangs), whereas Type 2 offenders target children as a result of a specific sexual interest in children (roughly equivalent of pedophile rings). CEOP found that 75% of Type 1 offenders were of Asian ethnicity, whereas 100% of Type 2 offenders were white."

Again the research confirms that grooming gangs are predominantly Asian. But how many Type 1 and how many Type 2 offenders are there? "**Type 1 groups tend to be larger: the majority involve groups of four abusers, compared to Type 2 abusers, who tend to act in pairs. That means in terms of raw figures, there are more Asian men carrying out group abuse than white men (229 compared to 70).**"

It can be expected that in terms of victims, the Asian grooming gangs also have more victims per perpetrator, compared to a pair of white pedophiles.

The comparison with pedophiles becomes odd when we recognize that the Asian gangs focus on girls that have (just about) hit puberty. Moreover, the vast majority of pedophiles do not operate in pairs, let alone groups. Most of them are lone wolves that prey on someone within their vicinity, someone they know and have access to. The Asian gangs, working in kebab shops and driving a taxi around town, have access to all local, vulnerable girls. [12]

Crimes where the victim is familiar with the perpetrator, like an uncle or family friend, are not less severe than those committed by strangers. However, people feel like they have some degree of control over such crimes when they hear about them on the news. They control who enters their house. When it comes to Asian gangs, anyone engaging in life and going to the heart of the town becomes a possible victim. Anyone could be the victim, and there is not much you can do as a parent.

Crime in Pakistan

Gruesome crimes in Pakistan aren't very rare either. An article from 2020 tells us, "A 5-year-old girl in southern Pakistan was raped, hit on the head and set on fire. Five days later, a woman in the country's east was dragged from her car and sexually assaulted on a highway in front of her children. The two episodes, which occurred hundreds of miles apart, have prompted protests and an outpouring of rage in a country that critics say has a toxic culture surrounding sexual assaults and child abuse."

Could it be that this toxic culture is brought over from Pakistan to the United Kingdom? "Ms. Aziz said that most of the child rape and abuse victims come from small towns or villages, and their cases do not usually catch fire on social media. Officials generally do not visit them either, she said, and perpetrators are often quietly released after public outrage has subsided — lending a sense of impunity after the crimes." Could it be said that Pakistan knows a 'rape culture'?

The New York Times continues with more detail on the two crimes. "The girl was kidnapped last Friday after going to buy cookies at a shop in the southern port city of Karachi, the police said. Her body was found two days later, and an autopsy indicated that she had been sexually assaulted. The police have arrested more than 20 suspects in the case, and investigators said on Wednesday that one had admitted to kidnapping and murder. In the second case, the woman was driving late Tuesday night with her three children from Lahore, the provincial capital of Punjab Province, to the city of Gujranwala, when her car ran out of fuel. She called the police, and as she waited for assistance, two men, both believed to be in their 30s, broke the driver's-side window with sticks and stones and dragged her and her children off the road. The woman was raped multiple times, and the men stole her A.T.M. cards, jewelry and cash, the police said. The Lahore police chief, Muhammad Umar Sheikh, later said that an extensive search for the culprits was underway. But the police chief also appeared to blame the woman for the crime, questioning why she had been traveling late at night without an adult male companion, and why she had not checked to see that her car had enough fuel for the journey."

It is worth noting that in both crimes the perpetrators were a group of multiple men, responding immediately when an opportunity was presented. Not a weird lone individual with devious thoughts, but something that appears to be quite culturally acceptable. A culture where two men can see a vulnerable woman and agree that it would be a pleasant experience for them to rape her together. Two men that likely were not hanging out together because they were both rapists, but both recognized the 'value' of the opportunity. [13]

During the first half of 2020, an average of six children per day were sexually assaulted. Almost one child was gang raped per day during the same period. Not only has gang rape in general been near inexistent in Europe before the wave of migration flooded it, gang raping children is one step even further. [14] Some of the children were found murdered after the gang rape had taken place.

Although the problems in the Catholic Church have been opened, discussed, and resolved, the problems in the Pakistani madrassas, their religious schools, go widely unnoticed and unaddressed. The situation is comparable in many ways to the Catholic situation, with Islamic clerics denying the allegations as blasphemy. Another sign that Pakistani culture is not yet developed, or might never develop, into a direction where they break away from the 'rape culture' that persists up to this day. Why do I say it may never develop? Because there is no guarantee that a culture moves in a certain direction. [15]

Terror Attacks

On 07/07 2005 Islamist terrorists bombed the London Underground, as well as a double-decker bus. Over 50 people died, with hundreds more being injured. The attack was claimed by Al-Qaeda and perpetrated by Hasib Hussain, Mohammad Khan, Shehzad Tanweer, and the Jamaican Germaine Lindsey who changed his name to Abdullah Jamal. It was the start of Islamic terror in the United Kingdom. Unfortunately, it wasn't the end.

In 2007 the Glasgow airport was attacked by Bilal Abdullah and Kafeel Ahmed. Several people were injured. In 2010 Stephen Timms, a member of parliament for the Labour Party was stabbed in an attempted assassination by Roshonara Choudry, an Islamic extremist.

In 2013 Lee Rigby was murdered by two Nigerians that had converted to Islam. Their names were Michael Adebolajo and Michael Adebowale. They said they killed him to avenge the killings of Muslims in the Middle East. Rigby had served in the UK military, and had fought in Afghanistan. Now, he was hacked and slashed to death, while the perpetrators tried to behead him. The two Nigerians remained on the scene, threatening others and celebrating their kill.

In 2017 Khalid Masood drove a car into a group of people and continued on a stabbing spree afterward. Six people died in the incident, which was claimed by the Islamic State. Under the victims were a mother on her way to pick up her children from school, an American visiting London to celebrate his 25th anniversary with his wife, and a Romanian tourist whose boyfriend had planned to propose to her during their trip to London. Out of nowhere, their lives ended.

Also in 2017 was the Manchester bombing at an Ariana Grande concert. The assailant was called

Salman Abedi. More than twenty people died in the attack. Nearly half of the ones that died were under twenty years old. The youngest was an eight-year-old girl. Dozens more children were brought to nearby hospitals for treatment. Salman Abedi had Libyan roots, his parents had migrated to the United Kingdom as refugees, fleeing the regime of Gaddafi. Clearly, he wasn't grateful for receiving the opportunity to live in the safety of the United Kingdom. He preferred to turn the United Kingdom into a warzone as well.

Again in 2017, Khuram Shazad Butt, Rachid Redouane, and Youssef Zaghba attacked on the London Bridge. They killed eight people and injured dozens more. All three died during the attack. The motive was, as always, Islamic extremism. One of the highlights from the event was the resistance by the local British inhabitants, where a baker threw a crate at the assailants, and a pub-goer took them on in a fist fight, shouting "Fuck you, I'm Millwall!"

Just months later, still 2017, Ahmed Hassan bombed the London Underground again, though failed in killing anyone. Still, dozens of people were injured for burn wounds. His motive was Islamic extremism.

In 2018 Salih Khater tried to ram several people with his Ford Fiesta at Westminster. He also failed in killing anyone, and, also, was motivated by Islamic extremism. At the end of the year Mahdi Mohamud stabbed multiple people at the Manchester Victoria station, he failed to kill anyone, but was heard shouting "Allah Akbar!"

In 2019, the UK witnessed another Islamic inspired attack. "Samiulahaq Akbari, 22, who arrived the UK in 2016 after fleeing Afghanistan, was yesterday jailed for 19 years with an extended license period of two years. Security camera video on January 8 shows Akbari walking into the supermarket in Thornton Heath, south London behind customer Nicholas Speight. He taps on Mr Speight's shoulder and asks of his nationality. Shortly after Mr Speight told him that he was from the UK, Akbari took out a 10-inch kitchen knife and attempted to stab at the victim."

So we have an asylum seeker, eager to flee the war and violence in Afghanistan, that goes out of his way to ensure that his victim is actually English. As great as it is to show hospitality and allow others access into your home, your land, there are rules for the guests as well. Trying to kill your host tends to be considered inappropriate, and rather rude. [16]

Later in 2019 Usman Khan killed two people and wounded another three in a knife attack on London Bridge. Khan had been previously convicted for terrorism and sentenced to several years in jail. Upon his release, he was celebrated as a showcase for rehabilitation. It appears that Khan was not so appreciative of his rehabilitation program, as the two people he killed were involved with his rehabilitation. He knew these people and had, so they thought, befriended them. "Both Saskia and Jack were involved with Learning Together, a prison rehabilitation charity, which was hosting the event at Fishmongers' Hall on November 29." Both were killed by Khan. [17]

UK Recap

The United Kingdom sees a clear overrepresentation of black and mixed-race ethnic groups, according to their own government data, when it comes to every type of crime. The overrepresentation is similar to that of the black ethnic group in the Netherlands who we have referred to as the Dutch Caribbean.

When we compare global crime statistics, it is clear that crime rates in the African Sub-Saharan homeland are far higher than the European average as well. It then appears that these violent and criminal attitudes are brought over to Europe alongside the flow of immigrants.

The second major group of immigrants in the United Kingdom, those from India and Pakistan, are not overrepresented in crime in general. For the groups of Indians, we find no clear indicator of any increased type of violence and criminality; however, the Pakistani group stands out when it comes to grooming gangs, where they form a near exclusive majority. Again, we find that this rape culture, lacking all respect for women, especially 'infidel' white women, matches with the culture we find in their home country of Pakistan.

Eastern European migrants show a smaller increase in crime, but are difficult to differentiate when they are grouped together with the white British population. Still, it is likely that their effect on crime is similar to that in the Netherlands, where it mostly affects theft, with minor increases in crime rates when it comes to other types of crime.

"Who controls the past controls the future. Who controls the present controls the past."

— George Orwell

Notes:

[1]
https://www.crimesecurityandsociety.org.uk/article/id/461/

[2]   https://theconversation.com/immigration-and-crime-is-there-a-link-93521

[3]
https://assets.publishing.service.gov.uk/government/uploads/system/uploads/attachment_data/file/669094/statistics_on_race_and_the_criminal_justice_system_2016_v2.pdf

[4]   https://www.bbc.com/news/uk-england-south-yorkshire-45980210

[5]
https://www.thesun.co.uk/news/4302003/rotherham-sex-abuse-scandal-child-grooming-exploitation-sarah-champion-mp/

[6]
https://www.thesun.co.uk/news/4299167/corbyn-ally-shares-message-telling-rotherham-sex-abuse-victims-to-be-quiet-for-the-good-of-diversity/

[7]   https://www.independent.co.uk/news/uk/home-news/grooming-child-sex-abuse-exploitation-rotherham-rochdale-police-a9215261.html

[8]   https://www.examinerlive.co.uk/news/local-news/i-raped-rotherham-grooming-gang-18121059

[9] https://www.bbc.com/news/uk-england-south-yorkshire-46368991

[10] https://www.theguardian.com/commentisfree/2018/nov/11/84-per-cent-of-grooming-gangs-are-asians-we-dont-know-if-that-figure-is-right

[11] https://news.sky.com/story/grooming-gang-convictions-84-asian-say-researchers-11164589

[12] https://www.channel4.com/news/factcheck/what-do-we-know-about-the-ethnicity-of-sexual-abuse-gangs#:~:text=CEOP%20assesses%20that%20type%201,longstanding%20sexual%20interest%20in%20children%E2%80%9D.

[13] https://www.nytimes.com/2020/09/11/world/asia/pakistan-rape-5-year-old-lahore-karachi.html

[14] https://www.thenews.com.pk/latest/713336-child-sexual-abuse-cases-shot-up-in-first-half-of-2020-in-pakistan-report

[15] https://www.newindianexpress.com/world/2020/apr/18/shocking-revelations-of-child-sex-abuse-in-pakistani-madrasas-2131916.html

[16] https://www.mirror.co.uk/news/uk-news/afghan-asylum-seeker-desire-kill-18941087

[17] https://www.mirror.co.uk/news/uk-news/family-london-bridge-attack-victim-21076852

Scared in Spain

"The truth may be stretched thin, but it never breaks, and it always surfaces above lies, as oil floats on water."

— *Miguel de Cervantes Saavedra*

Spain, the shortest trip from Africa to Europe brings you straight to Spain. The lacking social benefits compared to other European countries means that for most migrants Spain is not the final destination. Spain's colonies were mostly in the Americas, which brings an additional though uncommon migration flow.

Rape

"Six African **migrants gang-raped a 12-year**-old girl in a small town near Madrid, but Spanish authorities kept information about the crime hidden from the public for more than a year, apparently to avoid fueling anti-immigration sentiments.

On March 15, 2018, the 12-year-old girl was playing in a park in Azuqueca de Henares with several other girls when, at around one o'clock in the afternoon, six migrants — five Moroccans and one Nigerian — approached the playground. They carried two of the girls off to a nearby abandoned building, but then let one of them go after discovering that she was a Muslim. The migrants, aged between 15 and 20, grabbed the 12-

131

year-old by her arms and legs and took turns raping her, first anally and then vaginally, for nearly an hour." [1]

It is worth highlighting here that first, once more a gang rape took place where a group of men target a young and vulnerable girl. Second, they clearly targeted a non-Islamic Spanish girl, intentionally letting the Muslim girl go, despite all the risks that would bring along with it.

Spain, like many other countries, does not keep data on crime in relation to nationality or migrant background. One statistic that is available is that of prison inmates. There, two groups are highly overrepresented.

"The official Spanish statistics agency (Instituto Nacional de Estadística, INE) shows that immigrants comprise roughly 10% of the overall Spanish population, but 32% of the Spanish prison population. The INE does not break the statistics down by the nationality of the inmates, although Interior Ministry data show that the majority of immigrants arrested in 2017 were from just two countries: Romania (18,032) and Morocco (17,464)."

Romanians tend to stand out in crime statistics, mostly due to the tendency of Roma gypsies to commit theft and burglary. Moroccans are hardly a surprise, they stand out in every single country where we have data.

Anecdotal Evidence

With hard data lacking, we can still observe the anecdotal evidence, which is plentiful. "In Barcelona, for example, 15 members of a North African itinerant crime gang known as 'Allah's Wolfpack' sexually assaulted a woman at a metro station. The migrants, some of whom are unaccompanied minors and all of whom are in Spain illegally, had long rap sheets and were well known to the police.

The attack, which occurred in the Barcelona suburb of Santa Coloma on November 11, 2018, took place when a couple attempted to exit the Can Peixauet subway station. The youths, from Morocco and Algeria, hurled insults and verbal abuse at the couple as they walked off a train, then followed the pair into an elevator, where they assaulted the woman and stabbed her male companion.

Police later found the youths in a nearby abandoned building, where they had been squatting for months, and where they had previously been arrested in connection with a series of robberies in the area. Police also said the youths were infected with scabies, which required police to activate a special decontamination protocol for the officers involved, the police vehicles and the jail cells. Eight of the 15 youths have since been released from police custody and are back on the street."

Shockingly, the majority of the perpetrators are already released and back on the street. One can wonder whether such people will truly change their beliefs and behaviors, or if it is a matter of time before they strike again.

"Alicante, April 16. Three Algerians gang-raped a 19-year-old woman. One of the men was arrested at the Alicante airport while trying to flee the country."

"Tarragona, March 28. Eleven underage migrants were arrested for gang-raping a girl at the Roman amphitheater. Of the 11, only one was remanded in custody." It may be estimated that they are once again free and roaming the streets, because it is difficult to sentence minors. The question remains whether these men were truly underage, or gave false birth dates in order to be seen as a child refugee, increasing the likelihood of being allowed to stay in the country. A not so uncommon practice.

"Alicante, March 26. Four underage Moroccans gang-raped an underage girl. They filmed the rape and then demanded that the girl pay 50 euros to avoid having the video posted online." How ruthless must one be to demand money and commit extortion for such a negligible amount, after committing such a horrendous crime?

"Alicante, March 22. Ten Algerians were arrested for gang-raping three girls aged between 14 and 17. Police said that the gang members sustained themselves by robbing homes and businesses and later selling the stolen items on the black market."

"Sabadell, February 2. Eight Moroccans gang-raped an 18-year-old woman in an abandoned warehouse. The woman was celebrating her birthday when she became separated from her friends. The Moroccans, aged between 21 and 53, were homeless and squatting in the warehouse. Of the eight, only two were remanded in custody."

"Algeciras, January 6. Three Dominicans were arrested for gang-raping a 14-year-old girl."

"Benidorm, January 5. Four Ecuadorians were arrested for drugging and gang-raping a 19-year-old woman on New Year's Eve."

The trend is clear. Groups of migrant men targeting young girls.

"Barcelona, May 18. A 36-year-old Dominican drug dealer was arrested for raping a 13-year-old girl in the Raval district."

"Valencia, May 16. A Bolivian man was arrested for repeatedly raping his 14-year-old daughter."

"Granada, April 17. A 45-year-old Moroccan man was arrested after masturbating in front of children during a Holy Week procession." Perhaps the Moroccan was offended by the display of Christian piety?

"Salt (Girona), April 4. A 42-year-old Malian man was arrested for sexually abusing his 14-year-old daughter."

"Hospitalet de Llobregat, March 11. A 25-year-old Indian man was arrested for raping an underage girl he had groomed on social media."

"Sagunto (Valencia), February 23. A 24-year-old Ecuadorian man charged with repeatedly raping a 16-year-old girl..." The man claimed to be the reincarnation of Jesus Christ.

"Berga (Barcelona), February 18. A 33-year-old Senegalese migrant was arrested for sexually assaulting a 72-year-old woman." Yes, you read her age correctly. The girls are not always young.

"Barcelona, February 7. A 40-year-old imam at a mosque was charged with anally raping a 13-year-old boy during a Koran lesson." As we mentioned when discussing Pakistan, madrassas are hotbeds of pedophilia just as much as the Catholic Church was.

"Blanes (Girona), February 6. A 24-year-old Senegalese migrant was arrested for sexually assaulting an 11-year-old girl."

"Beniel (Murcia), February 5. A 34-year-old Moroccan man was arrested after he grabbed the breasts of two girls at an outdoor festival."

"Sant Josep (Ibiza), February 2. A 48-year-old Moroccan was arrested for sexually assaulting an 87-year-old woman in her home. The man broke into her home and after verifying that she was alone, he threw her to the ground and sexually assaulted her. The woman suffered severe trauma to her face. Police said the same man had sexually assaulted a 19-year-old woman in nearby Sant Antoni in April 2018." Apparently the man has no age limits on either bound.

"Leganés, January 28. A Pakistani man was arrested for sexually assaulting two teenage girls in his home. The man lured the girls by placing false advertisements in which he said he was looking for child care and housecleaning services."

"León, January 19. A Senegalese migrant was arrested for soliciting the prostitution of a 16-year-old girl. He offered her money and asked how much she charged per night."

"Santomera (Murcia), January 15. An Algerian man was arrested for making sexual propositions to a group of children and inviting them to his home."

"Valencia, January 12. A Colombian man was arrested for drugging a 16-year-old girl and attempting to rape her."

"Valencia, May 17. An 18-year-old Moroccan was arrested for raping an 18-year-old Belgian tourist."

"Madrid, May 10. A 27-year-old Guinean man was arrested for sexually assaulting three woman at a night club in Carabanchel."

"Martorell, May 9. A 40-year-old Moroccan man was arrested for attempting to rape three women who were jogging along the banks of the Llobregat River. A local judge sent the man to a mental health clinic."

"Barcelona, April 19. A 32-year-old French citizen of Moroccan origin raped a 37-year-old Portuguese woman in the gardens of the Maritime Museum, located just off La Rambla, one of the top tourist attractions in Barcelona. The rapist bit off his victim's ear, broke her arm and left her badly bruised. Police delivered the severed ear to a local hospital, where doctors performed reconstructive surgery. A week before the attack, local residents had alerted police to the man's aggressive behavior. He was arrested three times and released. Some believe that with stricter law enforcement, the attack could have been prevented."

"Murcia, April 15. Two Moroccans, aged 21 and 26, were arrested for kidnapping and sexually assaulting an 18-year-old transsexual."

"El Vendrell (Tarragona), April 8. A 23-year-old Dominican man was arrested for raping a 32-year-old woman in the entrance to her apartment building."

"Crevillent (Alicante), March 5. A 32-year-old Moroccan man was arrested for stalking and sexually assaulting several women on city streets."

"Bermeo, March 4. A sub-Saharan African attempted to rape a woman in the town center."

"La Palma del Condado (Huelva), February 27. A Romanian man was arrested for sexually assaulting two women in a public park."

"Lloret de Mar (Girona), February 23. A 23-year-old Moroccan man raped a woman in an ATM booth."

"Lorca, February 26. A 31-year-old Moroccan man attempted to rape a woman he ambushed from behind."

"Madrid, February 26. A 31-year-old Romanian man was arrested for sexually assaulting at least five women near the Tres Cantos railway station."

"Valencia, February 24. A 48-year-old Pakistani man attempted to rape a woman in a parking garage."

"Santa Cruz de Tenerife, February 22. A Moroccan man was arrested for sexually assaulting a woman in front of a refugee shelter. When the woman's boyfriend intervened, he was attacked with blows to the head."

"Pamplona, February 19. Three Romanians, aged 17 and 18, were arrested for sexually assaulting a woman in the restroom of a bar."

"Marbella, February 13. A 35-year-old Chinese man was arrested for sexually assaulting a woman on two separate occasions. Both times, the man tied the woman with a rope and gagged her. He beat her, sexually assaulted her and then used her cell phone to transfer money from her bank account."

"Beniaján (Murcia), February 12. A Moroccan man raped a 37-year-old woman he had met a few days earlier. In May, three men had also been arrested for gang raping a woman in the same town."

"Villaviciosa de Odón (Madrid), February 9. A 21-year-old Cameroonian man raped a 21-year-old British student. The man, who arrived in Spain as a political refugee, had received free housing and social assistance for a year while his asylum application was processed." Once more, are these the people we should help by inviting them to live among us, as our neighbors?

"Marbella, February 8. A Senegalese man attempted to rape a waitress at a restaurant. The man entered the establishment at around 11AM and began flirting with the woman, who told him that she was married. The man left. Shortly thereafter, she stepped outside to make some purchases at a nearby supermarket when the man ambushed her and tried to rape her."

"Cádiz, February 7. A 19-year-old Guinean migrant was arrested after he repeatedly flashed his genitals at passersby. Police said he was in the country illegally."

"Palma de Mallorca, February 4. A 42-year-old Moroccan man was arrested after he repeatedly grabbed the breasts of female passersby at the central train station."

"Capdepera (Majorca), January 22. A 25-year-old Moroccan man was arrested for sexually assaulting a 39-year-old woman who was riding her bicycle."

"Culleredo, January 21. A Peruvian man sexually assaulted a woman on a regional bus."

"Guadalajara, January 20. A 25-year-old Algerian man was arrested for attempting to rape a 40-year-old woman."

"Mataró, January 14. A Moroccan man sexually assaulted a woman in a parking garage."

"Valencia, January 9. A Lebanese man was arrested for drugging and raping a 20-year-old woman on New Year's Eve."

"Villajoyosa (Alicante), January 8. A 29-year-old woman was sexually assaulted at Hospital de la Marina Baixa by two men who appeared to be Moroccan. The hospital has been the scene of several sexual assaults: workers must walk along a dark road when going from the hospital to the parking garage."

"Mislata (Valencia), January 5. A 28-year-old Colombian drugged and raped a 16-year-old girl."

"Burriana (Castellon), January 2. Two Romanian men were arrested for kidnapping and raping a 17-year-old girl on New Year's Eve."

"Valencia, January 1. An 18-year-old Guinean sexually assaulted a female street cleaner."

Even where the immigrants and locals end up in relationships, integration doesn't necessarily take place. In Madrid a Moroccan man killed his fiancé, a Spanish woman, and fled to Morocco. He had 30 prior convictions - I don't know why he wasn't in jail either.

In Granada a Moroccan man stabbed his ex-wife. In Valencia a Moroccan man kidnapped his wife and daughters and physically assaulted them. In Tudela an Algerian man threatened to kill his wife. In Burriana a Moroccan man assaulted his daughter because she spoke to a male classmate.

In Totana an Ecuadoran beat and raped his girlfriend when she refused to have sex with him. In Reus, a Dominican man decapitated his wife. In Salamanca a Colombian man attacked his wife in the middle of the street.

In Murcia a Moroccan man attacked his wife and threatened to kill her after she requested a divorce. In Vigo a Moroccan man threatened to kill his wife for talking too much to the neighbors. In Salamanca a Moroccan man stabbed his pregnant wife. In Laredo an Ecuadorian killed his ex-girlfriend.

Underage unacompanied migrants are known as Menas in Spain, and Menas can commit crime as well. They have been known to punch a woman in the face, breaking her nose, in order to steal her phone. They have attacked their tutors and police officers. They try to rape their female tutors. A Moroccan Mena in Barcelona was convicted for the rape of six women, varying in age from 40 to almost 80 years old.

Somehow offenders, even when convicted, are quickly released back into society. I'm not sure what about Spanish law makes this permissible, but apparently it happens. A Moroccan man broke into seven cars in a single night, was arrested, had seventeen prior convictions, but was released.

An Algerian man was caught stealing a purse, and had more than 170 prior convictions. Another Algerian was arrested for breaking into at least twenty cars in a single week. An Algerian gang leader was arrested for the fourth time, his gang has committed hundreds of car thefts and burglaries. A Moroccan gang was caught stealing dozens of cars and reselling them in Africa.

Elderly people are not safe from the seemingly random violence. Two Moroccan men killed a 75-year-old woman when robbing her. An Algerian started beating a 91-year-old woman with a metal bar from a shopping cart. A Pakistani man assaulted and robbed a handicapped man. The judge gave him a suspended sentence for being a first-time offender. He was accused of robbing a woman several hours later.

A Moroccan man assaulted a couple, both over eighty years old, when robbing their home. Two Algerians, posing as plumbers, robbed the houses of dozens of elderly people. Another Algerian would offer to open the door, or carry the grocery bags, for elderly women as they returned home from the grocery store. He used this introduction to rob them.

In Madrid, two Dominicans were arrested for the murder of a twenty-year-old student during a fight at a festival. The Dominicans belonged to a gang that was dedicated to mugging people during festivals.

Two Moroccans were arrested after a seventeen-year-old was killed in a fight at a disco. A different Moroccan stabbed a woman when she refused to hand over her purse. A gang of Moroccan youngsters beat up a fifteen-year-old boy when he looked at a pair of girls from the group. That seems to have been little more than an excuse, as they have been harassing everyone in the area for months.

Again, a Moroccan man, illegally in Spain, was sentenced to one year in prison for assaulting a prostitute that refused to have sex with him for free. That's not quite how prostitution works, that's just rape.

In a different story, a Moroccan man kidnapped his own wife and demanded ransom. A Moroccan and a Dominican, both twenty years old, were arrested for stabbing another Dominican man in the neck. Sounds like attempted murder. In Tarragona, two Moroccans requested a pregnant woman that she'd hand over her backpack, when she refused, they kicked her in the stomach.

A Guinean man (some variety) robbed a woman of twenty euros and left her unconscious. A Moroccan, illegally in Spain and pending a deportation order, attacked a woman and stole her purse. When police intervened, he assaulted the police. Four Algerians and a Moroccan were arrested after assaulting a man that had just won over a thousand euros playing bingo.

In an asylum center near Madrid, unaccompanied minors attacked the security guards. On the beautiful island of Mallorca, unaccompanied minors sexually abused other refugees, and made threats to the staff working there.

Also in Mallorca, four migrants selling counterfeit goods attacked the police, threw the police officers on the ground, and kicked them in the head. In Murcia, an Algerian man tried to run over a police officer who asked him to stop for a routine traffic control. In Barcelona, a Moroccan man shouted "Allahu Akbar" and tried to stab several police officers. A Senegalese migrant broke a police officer's leg when they attempted to arrest him for stealing a phone.

Sentences for these violent criminals are low in socialist and progressive Spain. A Moroccan man who pleaded guilty with regards to raping a woman, was given a five year suspended sentence, provided he would not rape anyone in the next five years. The ruling was justified because the Moroccan had a cannabis addiction that diminished his intellectual capacity.

A Moroccan man that exposed himself repeatedly to an eleven-year-old girl was sentenced. He remains free pending appeal, as if there would be no risk of such a person actually raping someone. A Brazilian man received a sixteen month suspended sentence for ejaculating onto a girl in a city bus. He is forbidden from using public transportation for eight months.

Another Brazilian man received eight years in prison for raping a sixteen-year-old in the showers of a gymnasium. A Costa Rican man received eight years for sexually assaulting a thirteen-year-old who was babysitting his own two children.

A Guinean migrant was spared a prison sentence, despite admitting that he sexually abused two underage girls. A Senegalese migrant on Mallorca received four years for the attempted rape of a British tourist in the bathroom of a bar in Magaluf.

Mbaye

Just like in other countries, when someone in the group of migrants dies and the police are in any way involved, riots ensue. "Also in Madrid, hundreds of undocumented migrants from sub-Saharan Africa went on a rampage in Lavapiés, one of the most multicultural districts of the Spanish capital. The riots were the direct result of many years of extreme deference by Spanish officialdom toward illegal immigrants, and a sweeping failure to enforce the law — all, apparently, out of a fear of being accused of racism. The riots were triggered by false rumors that the local police had killed a 35-year-old Senegalese street hawker named Mmame Mbaye.

Spanish cities today are filled with illegal migrants from Africa who sell counterfeit merchandise on city streets. They are known as *manteros* (blanket men) for displaying their goods on blankets (*mantas*), and whenever the police approach, for scooping up the blankets and fleeing. Mbaye died, according to initial reports, after allegedly being chased by police from Puerta del Sol, in the city center, to Lavapiés, where he collapsed.

On April 22, 2019, however, a court in Madrid confirmed that Mbaye did not die as the result of a police chase. Instead, he had heart disease and died of cardiac arrest while walking with a friend in Lavapiés.

'The events do not reveal even the slightest indication that the deceased was personally subjected to any type of harassment or previous police persecution that could have triggered the lethal effects of the cardiac pathology from which he suffered,' the court ruled. 'There is no objective data or any witness to affirm the existence of such harassment or persecution, which has no support other than the mere assertions of the appellant [an NGO called SOS Racism Madrid]' Mbaye's death nevertheless sparked violent protests that lasted for several days and caused massive destruction of public and private property."

This story seems comparable to what has happened in places like France and Belgium, where the death of a migrant led to massive riots. It even resembles to some extent the death of George Floyd, bringing about the 'Black Lives Matter' movement. The groups of minorities cling together and support one another, whether or not supporting evidence to their claims exist. I will call out here that George Floyd's body showed signs of drug use, and nobody has been convicted for his death so far.

Research on Spain

A few researchers got their hands on some data with regards to nationality and crime in Spain. Their analysis showed that Africans had far higher homicide rates, both in Spain and in their home countries. The research was conducted by Cesar Alonso-Borrego, from the University Carlos III of Madrid, Nuno Garoupa, and Pablo Vazquez. The article comes from 2012 and is titled 'Does Immigration Cause Crime? Evidence from Spain.'

They had this to say, "At the same time, the differences across continents of origin can indicate that different nationalities represent a distinct attitude toward crime that might not have been eliminated by the process of integration."

Basically, they state that Africans have a cultural attitude towards crime, and that integration has failed to change that attitude.

Their conclusion says, "The present work introduces a first comprehensive analysis of the relationship between immigration and crime in Spain. In the context of the EU, Spain is not a country with high crime rates. During the last decade of significant immigration, Spain has seen an important rise in crime at a similar pace with its immigrant population but to a lower rate than other countries. We hypothesize that the explanation of this behavior is related to the individual characteristics of the immigrants that Spain has received. We argue that it is not so much the number of immigrants but the specific characteristics that seem to explain the relationship between crime and immigration in Spain. In this respect, cultural proximity and education must be specially noted. Immigrants from some populous groups, such as those who are Spanish native speaking, present a substantial proportion of people with at least secondary education, for whom criminality is much lower. This effect has contributed decisively to avoid any kind of explosion of criminality. Gender has also positively contributed to this effect. In fact, even after controlling for gender and education, we can still conclude that Latin-American immigration has probably undermined the potential rise of criminal rates in Spain. This result also happens, to a lesser extent, with EU15 immigrants. Our result is fully consistent with the evidence for the United States regarding Mexican immigrants (known as the Latino Paradox), where immigration from Mexico has lowered crime rates in some areas. Other immigrant groups with lower education levels have contributed significantly to the rise in crime rates. It must also be noted that these immigrants started at arrival with a crime rate significantly higher than Spanish nationals but have been converging as their size and composition changed. It must be noted the specific case of the Romanian immigrant group, now one of the most numerous in Spain. Even though it started with high crime rates, nowadays it presents lower rates than nationals in the 20–50 age group."

What they say in this conclusion is as important as what they don't say. They confirm the Spanish-speaking immigrants from South America have not negatively affected crime rates. They confirm that, beyond the early arrivals from Romania, European migrants have not significantly impacted crime rates.

Yet, they also say that immigrants have pushed crime rates upwards. This, clearly, implies the negative contribution of the African migrants. Both North-Africans and Sub-Saharan Africans are the 'uneducated' groups that are culturally distant, which push the crime rates up. Sadly, it appears that even when it comes to science, the scientists are afraid to actually say this, and prefer to leave it to the reader to pick up on it.

On a side note, the 'Latino Paradox' is no longer a paradox when you take into account that blacks in the United States, just like in the United Kingdom, just like in the Netherlands, have crime rates that are far above the rest of the population. So when Latino's migrate to culturally diverse neighborhoods, or in other words, neighborhoods with a large black population, they end up lowering crime in that area. [2]

Often people will deny that immigration leads to crime, referring to research done in the United States which showed that immigration actually reduced crime rates. However, you cannot compare the immigration of virtuous Latino's with immigration of uneducated Africans. I know multiple people that have migrated from South America to Spain, they tend to be people with Spanish ancestry, which gives them a right to relocate to Spain legally. These tend to be intelligent, educated people, taking on decent jobs. The whole reason they wanted to leave South America was the violence, poverty, and lack of opportunity. They are the virtuous people looking for a brighter future.

That is opposed to uneducated masses that seek easy money, vulnerable women, and a government that'll take care of them. Whenever we read any research on crime and immigration, we have to see to what extent they diversify the group of immigrants that they discuss. There is no point in reading a piece of research that combines all European, Asian, and African immigrants and treats them as if they are a homogenous group.

Denial

As is usual when presented with an inconvenient truth, there is plenty of denial that takes place. The Atlantic published an entire article, claiming there is no such thing as a problem with migrant crime. It defended its claims by stating that in one of the news reports, the perpetrators were falsely identified as Maghrebi, while actually being South Americans. The thing is, even if the report was false, that doesn't actually debunk the overall statement that migrants cause crime.

One, the anecdotal evidence goes beyond a single individual report. Two, the statistical evidence is taken from a large number of cases, where one single data point does not alter the outcome of the analysis. This is no more than building up a strawman, some easy argument to fight against. Disproving a single event, does not disprove the entire situation. [3]

And then the opponents may say, 'but it's not just a single event'. Other websites attack the flow of fake news that attacks the islamisation of Spain. They call it 'Islamophobia', an odd term considering nobody considers criticism on Christianity to be Christianophobia. The fear of Christianity is not even recognized by my spellcheck as an actual word, while Islamophobia is. It is not a fear of the religion, it is critique.

Anyway, the existence of fake news, even when it goes viral, neither proves, nor disproves what the situation is really like. A fake quote by an Arab immigrant saying he wants to kill Spaniards does not prove that Arabs are evil and dangerous. However, proving that the quote is fake does not prove that the conclusion is wrong either.

It just means that that single piece of 'evidence' is invalid and not worth discussing. That could settle the debate, if no further evidence exists. Yet, the evidence, both anecdotal and statistical is overwhelming. Moreover, the same evidence is consistently found in each and every European country.

> *"Virtue is persecuted by the wicked more than it is loved by the good."*
> — *Miguel de Cervantes Saavedra*

Notes:

[1]   https://www.document.no/2019/05/20/spain-surge-in-migrant-crime/
https://www.gatestoneinstitute.org/14249/spain-migrant-crime

[2]
https://www.researchgate.net/publication/230886154_Does_Immigration_Cause_Crime_Evidence_from_Spain

[3]
https://www.theatlantic.com/international/archive/2019/09/fake-news-feeds-anti-migrant-sentiment-spain/598429/

PORTUGUESE PENALTY

"Portugal was born in the shadow of the Catholic Church and religion, from the beginning it was the formative element of the soul of the nation and the dominant trait of character of the Portuguese people."
- Antonio de Oliveira Salazar

The smaller portion of the Iberian Peninsula. Portugal is somewhat out of the way for migrants coming to Europe. On top of that, it is a relatively poor country, with limited social benefits. Thereby, despite its proximity to Africa, immigration to Portugal has been limited.

No Data

Portugal, once more, does not track crime statistics based on ethnicity or race. "Direct or indirect registration by the state of data allowing for the identification of such information of such information is prevented by law in order not to reinforce stereotyping." The little research available tells us "A raw comparison between national and foreign residents seems to suggest a higher involvement of the latter in criminal behavior".

However, that only reviews those with Portuguese nationality, and those residing in Portugal without Portuguese nationality. Considering many immigrants have obtained their new nationality, and the effects of second-generation immigrants are not to be ignored either, this tells us very little. [1]

Portugal has not been the favorite immigrant destination. It's a poor country with a weak welfare state compared to Germany or Sweden. That, and the language barrier, may be one reason why I have failed to find a lot of information on crime caused by migrants in Portugal.

A secondary hypothesis could be found in an article written by the BBC, which says, "They treat us like animals," Sousa says of the police. "It's a black neighborhood - they treat us like we're all here to be exterminated." Apparently, the police in Portugal do not play games when it comes to the immigrant neighborhoods. Is that the key to a safe environment? [2]

It is worth noting that Portugal has a tiny Muslim population, which explains the lack of news headlines on gang rapes, terrorist attacks, and child grooming practices. [3]

Most immigrants in Portugal are instead Africans, generally there to work illegally in the vineyards. These groups do cause an increase in crime, though in Portugal especially it appears to be petty crime. Some fights, some increase in theft, and a little bit more chaos. However, compared to the rest of Europe the 'big crime' appears to have bypassed Portugal.

"Beggars innumerable, blind, dumb, and scabby followed me almost into the water. No beggars equal those of Portugal for strength of lungs, luxuriance of sores, profusion of vermin, variety and arrangement of tatters, and dauntless perseverance."

– William Beckford

Notes:

[1]
https://link.springer.com/chapter/10.1057/9780230283954_7

[2] https://www.bbc.com/news/magazine-32419952

[3] http://www.clovisinstitute.org/europes-growing-muslim-population/

ABOMINATIONS IN AUSTRIA

*"So many civilizations have come and gone on this land-
Celts, Romans, Normans, Mongols, French. Who knows
how many more?"*

– Karen Essex

Like Germany, but smaller and more mountains, plus they speak German in a funny accent. Still, Austria has a nice welfare state and is just as attractive to foreign immigrants. And so, it faces crimes that are similar to those in Germany.

Sexual Emergency

The most absurd headline that originated in Austria was that of the 'sexual emergency' rape in a swimming pool. The perpetrator, Amir, a recently arrived refugee from Iraq, raped a ten-year-old boy in the swimming pool. He pulled the boy into a cubicle, where he raped the boy.

As part of his defense, Amir claimed he did not know that the child did not consent. Apart from it being statutory rape regardless whether or not the boy consented, it is an outright absurd claim not to know whether or not a ten-year-old consented in order to get away with blatant rape.

"The court did not dispute the watertight evidence that some form of sexual abuse had taken place during the incident in a toilet cubicle at the Theresienbad swimming pool in December 2015. But in Austrian law, prosecutors must prove that an attacker is fully aware the act is nonconsensual for a more severe rape conviction to hold."

This section of Austrian law sounds like it was designed to prevent women from claiming it was rape after a night of drunken sex that they regret afterwards, not to protect a child rapist. Yet, in this perversion of the law, such legal mumbo jumbo is used to defend a foreign child rapist. A true abomination of justice.

The article continues, "As a relatively newly-arrived refugee, the trip to the swimming pool was organized as part of public integration efforts. The court heard how Amir dragged his victim into the cubicle, locked the door and raped him. The child reported the attack to a lifeguard, and when police arrived they found Amir had returned to the pool and was playing on a diving board, making no attempt to flee."

The trip to the swimming pool was organized in an effort to promote integration. Is it fair to say that this effort failed and was completely misguided? Clearly, Amir was granted a degree of trust that he didn't deserve.

"According to reports, Amir confessed to the attack in initial police questioning, telling them it had been a *sexual emergency* because he had not had sex for four months. In its initial sentencing, the court heard how the 10-year-old victim had suffered both physical and mental injuries in the attack, which amounted to serious bodily harm. The boy continues to suffer from post-traumatic stress disorder, his mother told the court."

The boy suffered severe anal injuries during the attack, for which he required hospital treatment. Now to just to highlight the absurdity here; Amir stated that it was a sexual emergency for having a four-month dry spell. That is, beyond all reasonable doubt, a completely crazy claim to make. But how does the court respond to it? "But in mitigation, judges cited Amir's own young age at just 20 when the crime was committed, his previous lack of convictions and his confession of responsibility."

The court takes into account Amir's 'confession of responsibility' when it determines the length of prison sentence. However, is it really confessing responsibility, when you say you experienced a sexual emergency and had no choice but to rape an underage boy? Moreover, how is Amir being a twenty-year-old any sort of mitigating factor? He is, quite frankly, a normal adult. Plus, it is odd that his previous lack of conviction is a factor at all, when he has only just arrived in the country. Shouldn't it be a more severe penalty for someone that just entered the country and immediately breaks the law? Do they even have access to the criminal records in his home country? [1]

In the end, Amir received a seven-year sentence. Only seven years, for raping a child and acting carelessly afterward. Either Amir is evil, or deranged and delusional, though in the end, those may be the same thing. It would appear that European courts are completely unequipped and unprepared to deal with these types of crimes.

The court system is built up in such a way that it gives people a second chance, it aims to reintegrate people into society. However, how useful is a court system aimed at reintegration, when the convicted felons were never integrated into society to begin with?

The boy's mother says he still screams at night, and despite being a refugee from Yugoslavia herself, she regrets telling her children to be welcoming to migrants. Do we all need to learn the hard way before we change our mind?

The pool is closed

The manager of another swimming pool has banned migrants from entering the pool unless accompanied by their social workers. This is not due to that single attack, but due to repeated misconduct on behalf of the migrants, followed by a continuous flow of complaints from the other bathers.

The migrants would follow women into the showers and the cabins to get dressed. Why do that? To be a pervert that gets off on watching women shower? Because you are looking for an opportunity to rape them? In order to sexually assault and grope them when nobody is looking? They would break open the vending machines and steal everything inside. They would steal from other guests.

The left-wing responded to the ban in protest, saying it was comparable to Nazi-Germany, and asking if only Aryans were allowed to take part in social life. Is that a measured and appropriate reply, or is it delusional and indicative of insanity? Why do they choose to ignore the crime and unrest caused by the migrants?

The left-wing politicians claim the actions of a few are used to stigmatize an entire group, using the migrants as scapegoats. I would like to ask them, how many constitute a few? It appears that the behaviors aren't as much 'incidental exceptions' as that they are consistent behaviors shown by large sections of the group.

It is furthermore odd to claim it makes the migrants into a 'scapegoat'. A scapegoat is someone that is "a person who is blamed for the wrongdoings, mistakes, or faults of others, especially for reasons of expediency." But they aren't blamed for wrongdoings, mistakes, or faults of others. They are blamed for wrongdoing by their own group. A scapegoat is appointing blame to someone that has no part in any of it, not someone that actually belongs to the group committing the crime. [2]

Scapegoats

If this book does anything, it will show that migrants are not used as scapegoats for crime statistics. It will show that it is not racism that leads people on Twitter and Facebook to ask "Who were the rapists?"

when another article on gang rape makes it to the headlines.

The New York Times discusses the crime wave in Vienna too, saying "By any measure, the string of crimes has been terrible. A grandmother of three, walking her dog, raped along a riverbank... A 21-year-old student gang raped near the giant Ferris wheel at Vienna's famed Prater park. A 54-year-old woman beaten to death on the street."

The grandmother was helped up a slope near a river by a young immigrant man who had recently arrived from Afghanistan. Then, the kind stranger changed his attitude, threw the grandmother to the ground, held her mouth with his hand, and tore off her clothes before raping her. In court, he denied the crime until the DNA evidence found on the grandmother confirmed his actions. He defended himself saying he had drunk a bottle of vodka and couldn't quite remember. The Afghan received twenty months, due to him having been a minor when he committed the rape. The grandmother's grandson had previously had his nose broken when a refugee punched him in the face.

The student getting raped was a Turkish girl, who got raped by three Afghans. Their lawyer stated that there are also many Afghans that integrate very well into Austrian society. A somewhat painful comment to make, when Afghans are overrepresented in crime statistics wherever they go.

The 54-year-old was a cleaner who was bludgeoned to death by a Kenyan man in the middle of the night, after she had finished her shift as a cleaner.

They continue, "The fact that the crimes were committed by recent migrants from war zones and an immigrant who had lived illegally in the country for years added an especially volatile element to the political climate ahead of the presidential election on Sunday, when Austria could become the first European country to elect a far-right candidate as head of state since the end of Nazism."

Apparently, any political party that says 'Hold on, wait a minute, these migrants sure are committing a lot of crime! Maybe we should stop this?' is a far-right party that can be compared to Nazism. The comparison, once more, is absurd. This is a political party that acknowledges immigration brings problems, and the New York Times immediately jumps to a Nazi reference. [3] The article doesn't go more in-depth with regards to the crimes, but laments how the crime wave may help the far-right candidate to win votes. That, it seems, is the real horror.

A similar trend is seen when it comes to Reuters, who published an article on the gang rape of a German woman visiting Vienna by nine Iraqi men. "Nine Iraqi asylum seekers and refugees have been arrested over the alleged gang rape of a 28-year-old German woman in Vienna on New Year's Day, Austrian police said on Monday, a case likely to fuel public debate over immigration and crime."

Immediately the horrible crime is glossed over and the discussion moves to how it will fuel the public debate over immigration and crime. I mean, isn't that what news articles are supposed to do? Aren't they supposed to fuel the public debate on that topic? Isn't news on climate change supposed to fuel the debate on climate change? It has this implied meaning of 'Let's not talk too much about this, it'll play into the hands of the far-right'.

The article has entire paragraphs dedicated to the political aspect, saying "The far-right Freedom Party, which is running first in opinion polls, has seized on cases in which immigrants have been accused of crimes to press for stricter immigration policies. Immigration is likely to be a central theme in the re-run of a presidential election on Oct. 2."

What does it mean that they 'seized on' such news articles? Does the Green Party 'seize on' articles relating to climate change in order to fit their agenda? Or do these political parties see what's going on in the world, and adjust their proposed policies to fit real world problems?

To make matters worse, Reuters clearly refers to the 'alleged' crime, highlighting how the woman was highly inebriated. This, at first glance, isn't too strange. And yes, it is factually correct to say it is an alleged crime, until someone has been convicted by a judge. Although, it must be added, they don't always choose to add such nuance.

Inebriation makes consent a little bit more complicated, as the question arises whether someone that is drunk can provide consent or not. This would apply to the case where a drunk guy takes a girl home from the pub, and she regrets it the next day. Was it rape? Opinions differ.

However, that is not quite the case here. Here, the woman was staying with a female friend. In the same building, some of the Iraqi perpetrators lived. So attempting to reach her friend, they pulled her into their apartment, where all nine had sex with her. There really is no moral explanation here.

The article implies that there is a possibility that the drunk woman got horny, saw the Iraqi refugees on her way to her friend, went home with them, and agreed to consensual sex with the entire group of men, ranging in age from her own age to twenty years her senior. Sure, it is possible that she was extremely horny, in the mood for a gang bang, and regretted it the next day. But is it likely? Is it a realistic scenario?

Besides, a question for all men reading this, who of you would see a drunk girl, and think it'd be a cool idea to have sex with her - not just you, but you and all of your friends. These opportunities may present themselves, but every guy I know would refuse it and consider it immoral, even when they'd believe they could get away with it.

The Reuters article ends with "The presumed perpetrators are likely to have taken advantage of the female victim's high level of inebriation," the Vienna police said in a statement. "The woman, from the northern German state of Lower Saxony, was celebrating at a square in central Vienna and does not remember what happened between about 2 a.m. and when she woke in the apartment around 6 a.m., the police spokesman said." The last words in the article sow doubt on what happened, and place blame on the victim. As if to say, well, she does not remember, so she may have consented. Because the fact that group sex had taken place isn't disputed. [5]

A later article from a different source shows a less ambiguous description of the events. "Four men took a heavily intoxicated German woman to an apartment where others were waiting to rape her. The men, some of whom had been granted refugee status, took turns raping the woman and took selfies with her."

Despite most of the men claiming it was consensual, or that they weren't there at all, one of the rapists confessed and offered an apology, knowing what they had done was wrong.

The woman had lost her friend in a crowd, and on her way home was taken by four men. They took her to an apartment where a further five men were waiting. The men took selfies of the victim, and had turns raping her. The group included a father and son. (What odd culture do you come from where it is an acceptable activity to rape a girl together with your dad?) The victim says she is highly disturbed and nothing makes her happy anymore. Understandable, after such a traumatic experience. [6]

Strangling

"A Syrian man who entered Austria posing as a teenager has been sentenced to 15 years in a secure unit for murdering his teen ex-girlfriend. Jazan A., 20, was found guilty by the court in the city of Wiener Neustadt in the Austrian state of Lower Austria where the body of his 16-year-old girl victim was found hidden under a bush in a park. The gruesome discovery was made by her own mother who went searching through town after the victim failed to arrive home from a night out with friends."

The Austrian girl had been in a relationship with the refugee, according to her mother it had been her first love. From the start, Jazan had tried to dominate the girl, easily becoming jealous and forbidding her to wear certain clothes. Jazan claimed innocence in the court, and has shown no remorse and has offered no apology.

He first lured her to the park, saying he wanted to meet her there to talk. There, he took out his belt and strangled her. The dead body was hidden under some twigs and leaves. Jazan, in another strange twist of justice, was spared prison and instead sent to psychiatric treatment for supposedly having a split personality. Still, his freedom is taken away for the next fifteen years. The question remains, is Jazan really a crazy lunatic, or did he do what his culture expects him to do? [4]

It is not the first time an Iraqi immigrant is convicted in Europe for murdering his ex-girlfriend. A similar case took place in Sweden in 2020, where a seventeen-year-old girl was decapitated. [7]

An Afghan refugee killed his ex-girlfriend in Germany by stabbing her. [8]

A Nigerian refugee in Germany murdered his ex-girlfriend, stabbing her to death, after jealousy took hold of him when she left him. [9]

In Berlin, a Tunisian asylum seeker stabbed to death his pregnant ex-girlfriend. After stabbing her, he calmly walked outside, telling her neighbors that they merely had a fight. [10]

I do not intend to claim that Europeans never murder their ex, but is it common or highly exceptional? Does it follow the same trend of simple jealousy that it does in all of these cases? Is it as common in Europe as it is in their Islamic home countries? I doubt it, but if there is evidence proving me wrong, I would love to see it.

Terrorism

For a long time Austria had been spared the kind of terror attacks that hit Germany, France, Spain, and the United Kingdom. Though in December 2020, an Islamic terrorist with an automatic rifle opened fire in a nightlife area, killing four people. Eventually, the terrorist was shot down by police.

"The gunman had already served a prison sentence for trying to go to Syria to join Islamic State jihadists, but he was released early because of his youth."

Once more, the European judicial system cannot cope with underage radicalism. Their aim for reintegration and mild punishment for 'children' has led to death and destruction once again.

"Nehammer [a politician] said the attacker had managed to fool a deradicalisation organization - a claim the organization has denied. However, he did admit that intelligence services failed to communicate information from Slovakia, that the attacker tried to buy ammunition there." The organization can deny that he fooled them all they want, but it is clear beyond doubt that he was not deradicalized. [11]

Statistics

In Austria 16% of the population are foreigners. Those that are living in Austria, but do not have an Austrian passport. The group thus excludes those with a migration background that have since acquired Austrian citizenship, as well as children born to parents with a migration background. Still, this 16% of the population makes up more than 40% of those suspected of, and convicted for a crime. [12] A trend that has been rising year over year since at least 2012, where it was close to 30%.

These foreigners are for a large part Germans and other surrounding countries, but Syrians and Turks are also a part of the top ten. [13] The trend in rising crime by foreigners isn't too strange when taken into account that foreigners as a percentage of the population have risen from 10% in 2011 to 17% in 2021. Still, they are vastly overrepresented in crime statistics. [14]

The same becomes apparent when we look at who's in prison. More than half of the prison inmates were foreigners, those without Austrian citizenship. Despite the vast majority of foreigners being immigrants from EU member states, those from outside of the EU formed a larger group in prison.

In September 2020, there were 2822 non-EU citizens in Austrian prisons. Only 1464 of those from EU member states were in prison, and more than 4000 with the Austrian nationality. However, once more, those with Austrian nationality include all those with a migration background. Numbers for native Austrians are thus even lower.

In other words, 33% of the prisoners in Austria are non-EU foreigners. I don't have full visibility as to the exact breakdown of nations of origin of all foreigners in Austria, but going by the top ten, where only four countries are non-EU, namely Turkey, Bosnia, Serbia, and Syria. Depending on which nations fill up the rest, between 6 and 9% of the total population consists of non-EU foreigners, responsible for 33% of the prison inmates.

Afghans, despite forming a small population group, are in the top ten of nationalities most often arrested. [16] Afghans, forming only 3% of the group of foreigners, are responsible for nearly 6% of crimes committed by the total group of foreigners. They are overrepresented within the group that is overrepresented. [17]

A piece of research written by professor Christian Grafl shows similar conclusions for Austria. Whereby foreigners, or 'fremden', formed 19% of the total population in his review, they formed 39% of suspects, 41% of those convicted, and 55% of the inmate population. [18]

Despite many countries seeing a downward sloping trend in overall crime statistics, Austria's has been on the rise since 2015, the year that the most non-Western immigrants arrived in Austria ever. [19] The increase in crime applies to all crime, as well as to severe crimes such as murder.

In 2018, in a general survey, 70% of the Austrians answered they believe immigration has a negative effect on crime. [15] How on earth could they have come to that conclusion? Are all Austrian racists, longing back to the time where Hitler annexed them? Alternatively, do they simply possess common sense and recognize what is going on around them?

"We are not against immigration, but we want to have control on immigration. We want to decide who is allowed to come into Austria. We should not let human traffickers decide."

-   Sebastian Kurz

Notes:

[1]
https://www.independent.co.uk/news/world/europe/
austria-swimming-pool-rape-theresienbad-vienna-
iraqi-refugee-a7473441.html

[2] https://www.youtube.com/watch?v=48AyV3hdewM

[3]
https://www.nytimes.com/2016/05/22/world/europe
/migrant-crimes-add-volatile-element-to-austrias-
election.html

[4]   https://austriametro.com/syrian-imposter-given-
15yrs-for-killing-teen-ex-gf/

[5]   https://www.reuters.com/article/us-europe-
migrants-austria-rape-idUSKCN10Q1GJ

[6]   https://www.dw.com/en/eight-iraqi-men-found-
guilty-of-gang-raping-german-woman-in-austria/a-
37783852

[7]   https://www.dailymail.co.uk/news/article-
8331341/Swedish-girl-17-decapitated-Iraqi-born-
boyfriend.html

[8]   https://www.rferl.org/a/failed-afghan-asylum-
seeker-jailed-8-1-2-years-in-germany-for-murder-of-
ex-girlfriend/29468054.html

[9]   https://www.dailymail.co.uk/news/article-
4791514/Asylum-seeker-killed-German-girlfriend-
jealousy.html

[10]
https://www.express.co.uk/news/world/754258/Tunisian-asylum-seeker-accused-stabbing-pregnant-ex-girlfriend-Berlin

[11]   https://www.bbc.com/news/world-europe-54838016

[12]
https://de.statista.com/statistik/daten/studie/917904/umfrage/auslaenderkriminalitaet-in-oesterreich/

[13]
https://de.statista.com/statistik/daten/studie/293019/umfrage/auslaender-in-oesterreich-nach-staatsangehoerigkeit/

[14]
https://de.statista.com/statistik/daten/studie/293102/umfrage/auslaenderanteil-in-oesterreich/#professional

[15]
https://de.statista.com/statistik/daten/studie/937148/umfrage/kriminalitaet-durch-zuwanderer-in-oesterreich/

[16]
https://de.statista.com/statistik/daten/studie/975823/umfrage/ermittelte-tatverdaechtige-in-oesterreich-nach-staatsangehoerigkeiten/

[17]
https://www.praeventionstag.de/dokumentation/download.cms?id=2769&datei=11-Grafl-2769.pdf

[18]
https://www.praeventionstag.de/dokumentation/download.cms?id=2769&datei=11-Grafl-2769.pdf

[19]
https://www.macrotrends.net/countries/AUT/austria/murder-homicide-rate

GRIM PROSPECTS IN GREECE

"In a democracy the poor will have more power than the rich, because there are more of them, and the will of the majority is supreme. It is also in the interests of a tyrant to keep his people poor, so that they may not be able to afford the cost of protecting themselves by arms and be so occupied with their daily tasks that they have no time for rebellion."

— Aristotle

The ancient cradle of democracy. Birthplace of Socrates, Plato, Aristotle, and with a bit of leniency even Alexander the Great. Genetically, modern Greeks are remarkably similar to those ancient Greeks that farmed the lands and planted the olive trees. Will this hold true in another two-thousand years?

Migrant Camps

Greece forms the entry point into Europe for many immigrants from Africa and the Middle East. There, the immigrants are put in camps on the islands, waiting for their passage into the richer part of Europe. Greece has neither jobs, nor free giveaways to offer. So what do you do when you have succeeded in fleeing your dangerous country, and have reached the safe lands of Europe? You may pray to God that you don't get COVID19, and your request may be granted. Then, someone stabs you.

"Whereas COVID-19 has yet to surface officially at the vastly overcrowded camp of Moria, five people have been murdered in knifings since the start of the year, including a woman and a young boy. Ten others have been injured." [1]

And why do they fight? Ethnic tensions, the same reason there is war in their home countries. "Tension between Afghanistan's ethnic Hazaras and Tajik are a frequent source of violence, says Nazifa, a teacher from that country."

She was asked whether she belonged to the Hazara or to the Tajik. Since she belongs to neither of those groups, both sides consider her an enemy. Once more, it appears that the groups of migrants take the war with them. War isn't bound to a geographic area, it's bound to the people that inhabit the area. It's people that kill each other, not rocks and sand.

Violence and crime starts at a young age. Four teenage Pakistani boys gang raped another teenage Pakistani boy, possibly from a different province or tribe. While the teenagers raped the boy, they also filmed it, highlighting that this was a crime of humiliation and entertainment. [21]

CNBC writes about the horrible conditions in the camp, after a protest by the migrants required riot police to be contained. They described the situation in the camp, and highlighted the murders taking place, as well as "Doctors Without Borders said that rape is also common inside the camp, as high as one rape reported a week." One rape every week, in a camp inhabited by around 20.000 people. That would make around fifty rapes a year, in a camp where at most half of the inhabitants are women, let alone adult women. Assuming there are 10.000 women in the camp, 0.5% of them get raped per year. And those are only the rapes that get reported, out of fear of repercussions many women likely keep their mouths shut. [2]

I mentioned 'adult' women, but it is clear that rapes are not restricted to those women only. A three-year-old Afghan girl was found raped and only half-conscious, covered in blood, in the camp's toilet. [4]

This wasn't the first time a young girl was raped in a migrant camp. Already in 2017 we can find reports of a four-year-old getting raped. Moreover, the article describes how other young girls are being raped as well.

"In one Greek camp, a man who had already married one child raped another underage girl, and was badly beaten by other migrants." Migrants resort to vengeful violence in these camps of chaos. "A man from one of the 'mafia' groups asked a couple's seven-year-old daughter into their tent to play games on his phone and then zipped up the tent," a doctor told researchers. "She came back with marks on her arms and neck. Later, the girl described how she was sexually abused."

The occasional rape, as bad as it is, dwarfs in comparison to the horrors of forced prostitution of underage girls. "Smugglers in Greece, Italy and elsewhere in Europe are known to force refugees including children into prostitution to pay debts, while migrants are also resorting to survival sex for food and shelter, or to raise money to leave Greece." This is the sad reality that those proponents of an open border policy refuse to see. [5]

Another difficulty is that the amount of rape may be even underreported. For women living in refugee camps, life is dangerous. If they go to the police, they may be beaten or stabbed by violent gangs. The reason most refugees travelling to Europe are men, is simply that it is too dangerous for women. It's not the weather or the journey that's dangerous, it's the groups of men that would accompany them.

Women without a partner or father to protect them, are easy targets for rape and to force into prostitution, so that their pimp can earn some extra income. A woman traveling on her own, would have to make a 'deal' with another man for protection. Unless she has large amounts of cash to offer, which most likely she won't, it isn't hard to guess what she'll use to bargain. It's better to have sex with one man in exchange for protection, than to be raped by entire gangs.

This is similar to the migrant stream running into the United States through Mexico, there estimates go as high as claiming that up to 80% of women taking this route are raped along the way. Rape is in fact such a common occurrence that female migrants will start taking contraceptives before setting out on their paths, calculating that they are likely to either get raped or be forced into sex in order to pay for a bribe. [20]

"In Athens, Thessaloniki and other cities, refugees tend to live in open camps or informal settlements, where adolescents may be preyed on by older men. Children desperate to raise money or find shelter also seek to sell sex themselves, particularly in notorious parks in Athens where they wait to be approached by pedophiles. The Harvard study found that the purchasers of migrant child sex were mainly men over 35, while children engaging in survival sex are mainly teenage boys, particularly from Afghanistan."

Such young boys that prostitute themselves are common in parts of Afghanistan and Pakistan. They're called 'Bacha bazi', boys to play with, or dancing boys. It is a form of institutionalized pedophilia, where older men have some fun with boys on the side. Women are for children, boys are for fun. The boys that take on this part, are those that are poor and vulnerable. It is a century-old practice that continues to this day. Now, alongside the immigrants, they seem to have brought this part of their culture along with them.

It is true that these migrant camps are filled beyond their planned capacity. However, that is not due to people fleeing war. When Turkey allowed a group of immigrants passage through their land, claiming they were refugees from Syria, it turned out that only 4% of the migrant batch consisted of Syrians. The percentage of Turks was 5%, while other groups included Pakistani and Moroccans pretending to be Syrians. [18]

Rapes

The desire to rape doesn't end at the boundaries of the migrant camp of course, so in Greece we see a trend very similar as to the rest of Europe. Aggressive stranger rape.

"The Afghan approached her and demanded to have sexual intercourse with her after threatening her with a knife, while at the same time he caused bodily injuries by hitting her in his attempt to subdue her resistance. However, he eventually failed to carry out his ill intentions." [6] Such attempts at rape won't even make it into the statistics, but are a life-changing situation nonetheless.

In a different episode, two men from Syria attempted to rape a twelve-year-old boy. [7]

A twenty-year-old Greek girl in Thessaloniki was gangraped by four Albanian Muslims. The Albanians fed her a cheap synthetic drug. [22]

One of the most horrible rape stories from Greece is that of a teenage girl called Myrto. She was fourteen years old at the time, when a Pakistani immigrant bashed her head in with a stone, and proceeded to rape her. She was in a coma for months, suffering severe injuries for which she received treatment in the United

States. The Pakistani claimed to be seventeen when he was arrested. This was a blatant lie, but he knows that this would've given him a more lenient sentence. [8]

A twenty three-year-old Greek woman and her boyfriend attended a refugee solidarity event. After the party, on their way home, they were ambushed by three men from Algeria and Syria. They were armed with broken glass bottles, and tied the pair up. Nearby, the solidarity event was still in full swing. The refugees threatened her, forced her to provide oral sex, and robbed her. [19]

Athens witnessed an attempted rape where a Pakistani man put a heavy chain around the woman's neck. "As the migrant attacker attempted to remove the woman's clothes, the chain loosened enough for the 54-year-old to grab a nearby object and hit the attacker on the head. The woman then ran outside into the street to call for help as the migrant fled the scene." [9]

In a different case, bearing similarities to the behavior of Pakistani grooming gangs in the United Kingdom, a Pakistani man had abducted two Greek teenage girls and kept them in his apartment. He fed them drugs, beat them up, and raped them. The girls were able to flee the apartment, and luckily ran into police officers on the street as the Pakistani man chased them. "The two girls complained that the man was holding them in a 5th floor apartment on Kerameikou Street, and with threats and violence forced the second girl into intercourse while he was beating the first one and threatening that he would kill them. We were informed that inside the apartment there was a quantity of drugs which he had for sale in the center of Athens." [14]

Another episode of Pakistani violence in Greece witnessed two Pakistani men kidnapping and raping a teenage boy. They forced the boy to call his uncle in Spain to send them money. They made footage of the boy naked and degraded, which they threatened to publish. [15]

Conquest

For the Greeks, this conflict is one part of a long history of conflict with its neighbor Turkey. Previously the Ottoman Empire, they used to rule Greece. "Erdoğan has repeatedly said that both this region of Western Thrace as well as the eastern islands most affected by the migrant crisis should be reconquered by Turkey, the imperial ruler of these borderlands until just over a century ago."

Erdogan seems eager to return to those days, and Greek instability is a win for Turkey. Although Turkish imperial desire sounds somewhat farfetched to those that believed we have surpassed history and the age-old tradition of conquering neighboring lands, it'd be good to remember that Turkey has invaded and holds to this day the northern half of Cyprus. They got away with it, because nobody cared to stop them. There were no international interests to protect when it came to

Cyprus, and Turkey formed a part of NATO, so nobody was inclined to aggrieve them. [3]

A paper written on illegal immigration in Greece by John M. Nomikos from the Research Institute for European and American Studies tells us, "Turkish governments are implementing the Ozal doctrine which says 'we do not need to make war with Greece. We just need to send them a few millions illegal immigrants from Turkey and finish with them.' The uncontrolled flow of illegal immigrants has multiple dangers for Greek national security because: i) it can destabilize social cohesion through demographic denaturation. ii) it encourages the spread of organized crime and terrorist networks. As an illegal immigrant, a high level operative of Al-Qaeda passed the Greek borders and was arrested by the Greek authorities since he tried with forged documents to receive political asylum." [23]

Jihad

Though Greece has been spared any terrorist attacks on its own soil, the country forms a gateway for wannabe-Jihadi's. "Police in the Greek capital of Athens have arrested a 27-year-old Syrian migrant who they say is an Islamic State jihadist involved in terrorist acts. The alleged jihadist was taken into custody by counter-terrorism forces at the Eleonas camp migrant camp where he was living with his wife and five children." [10]

Another known jihadist was arrested in the Greek city of Tripoli, where he had been living for several years. "According to Kathimerini, Tajikistan authorities consider him a high-ranking Islamic State official." [11]

In a different part of Greece, "A court in northern Greece has convicted a Syrian refugee of having been a fighter with the Islamic State group in Syria, and sentenced him to eight years' imprisonment." The man himself stated that he did not belong to the Islamic State, but had fought for the Free Syrian Army instead. [12]

Despite the inflow of clearly dangerous immigrants, the EU refused to support building a wall at the border with Turkey, which would have blocked the easiest entry point. The EU, however, does not believe in building walls. More likely, they would prefer to build a bridge between Europe and Africa. [13] Despite not wanting to fund a wall, the EU is willing to offer two thousand euro to migrants in order to return home. [16]

In an odd twist of fate, the Greek government pressed charges against an Afghan father, who made the crossing from Turkey to Greece. During the crossing, their boat capsized, and his six-year-old son died. According to the Greek government, it was a case of reckless endangerment, and the father failed in his parental duties to look after the safety of his son. After all, Turkey was already a safe country, so there was no imminent danger.

It is an interesting twist as the story is very similar to that of Aylan, the boy who made front-page news around the world and became a cause for open borders. About Aylan; nobody blamed his parents for taking such an unnecessary risk. "Father and son had been part of a group of 25 people who left Turkey hoping to claim asylum in Europe, but their boat, believed to be a dinghy, reportedly capsized in the Aegean Sea. The six-year-old's body was found on the shores of Samos near a pregnant woman, who was still alive and gave birth several days later." This is how propaganda and the way the mainstream media phrases events can change how people perceive reality. [17]

"The activities of the state are those of the rulers and those of the persons ruled, and the work of a ruler is to direct the administration and to judge law-suits; but in order to decide questions of justice and in order to distribute the offices according to merit it is necessary for the citizens to know each other's personal characters, since where this does not happen to be the case the business of electing officials and trying law-suits is bound to go badly; haphazard decision is unjust in both matters, and this must obviously prevail in an excessively numerous community."

- Aristotle

Notes:

[1] https://www.arabnews.com/node/1688191/world

[2] https://www.cnbc.com/2020/03/01/refugee-crisis-in-greece-tensions-soar-between-migrants-and-locals.html

[3] https://www.vice.com/en/article/3a8mny/what-the-hell-is-happening-with-migrants-in-greece

[4] https://www.barrons.com/news/greek-minister-defends-migrant-camp-safety-after-rape-incident-01608399904

[5] https://www.independent.co.uk/news/world/europe/refugee-crisis-trapped-greece-children-girl-raped-boys-selling-sex-prostitution-eu-athens-a7695971.html

[6] https://greekcitytimes.com/2020/09/25/illegal-immigrant-from-afghanistan-attempted-to-rape-woman-in-ioannina/

[7] https://greekcitytimes.com/2020/11/21/syrian-illegal-immigrants-rape/

[8]   https://greekreporter.com/2014/01/25/myrto-papadomichelakis-returns-to-greece/

[9]
https://www.breitbart.com/europe/2020/11/29/greek-police-hunt-for-migrant-chain-rapist-after-attack-on-54-year-old/

[10]
https://www.breitbart.com/europe/2020/11/21/greek-police-find-alleged-islamic-state-jihadist-in-migrant-camp/

[11]
https://www.breitbart.com/europe/2020/11/06/greece-arrests-islamic-state-migrant-helped-pro-migrant-ngos/

[12]
https://www.breitbart.com/europe/2018/03/19/greek-court-jails-syrian-asylum-seeker-islamic-state-membership/

[13]
https://www.breitbart.com/europe/2020/03/16/flas

hback-eu-refused-fund-pointless-greek-border-fence-
before-crisis-we-are-against-building-walls/

[14]   https://www.jihadwatch.org/2020/12/greece-
muslim-migrant-arrested-for-drugging-and-raping-
two-teen-minors

[15]
https://www.breitbart.com/europe/2020/07/25/paki
stani-migrants-sentenced-kidnapping-extorting-
raping-teen-greece/

[16]   https://www.bbc.com/news/world-europe-
51859007

[17]   https://www.theguardian.com/global-
development/2020/nov/16/father-faces-criminal-
charge-over-sons-death-in-migrant-boat-tragedy

[18]   https://www.vice.com/en/article/3a8mny/what-
the-hell-is-happening-with-migrants-in-greece

[19]   https://www.jihadwatch.org/2018/03/greece-
woman-goes-to-refugee-solidarity-event-gets-gang-
raped-by-muslim-migrants

[20]   https://www.huffpost.com/entry/central-america-migrants-rape_n_5806972

[21]
https://www.express.co.uk/news/world/716044/migrants-pakistan-gang-rape-boys-moira-greece-immigrants-asylum-seekers-sex-sexual-assault

[22] https://greekreporter.com/2014/02/05/20-year-old-greek-girl-claims-gang-rape/

[23] https://www.rieas.gr/images/rieas144.pdf

Notorious in Norway

"Either conform to the customs or flee the country."
– Norwegian saying

Norway, the Dubai of the north, the richest oil state of Scandinavia. Life is rich, but cold. The Norwegians decided to maintain their independence and refused to join the European Union. Although their borders are definitely not closed, they are overshadowed by the willingness of the Swedes to take in everyone.

Statistics

"Figures from Statistics Norway show that migrants are vastly overrepresented in crimes, with younger migrants especially involved in violent crime and abuse in Oslo. The figures were highlighted by Progressive Party members Sylvi Listhaug and Jon Helgheim, who revealed that young immigrant men from Somalia commit violent crime at a rate of 419 per 1,000 compared to 34 per 1,000 for native Norwegians."

Nearly half of young immigrant men from Somalia commit violent crime, compared to 3.4% for native Norwegians. The report shows us "that migrants are far overrepresented in violent crime even when factors such as gender, age, social status, and employment status are taken into consideration." [2]

Somalians from the second generation of immigrants, those born in Norway to Somalian parents, continue to be highly overrepresented in crime, committing nearly five times as many crimes as their Norwegian native counterparts. [5]

In Norway, the most damning piece of evidence is that 95% of stranger rapes are committed by non-Western immigrants. Norway keeps track of violent street rape as a separate category, a category where non-Western immigrants are consistently overrepresented. [1]

In Oslo immigrants make up around one third of the population of the city, though they account for nearly 70% of violent crime. A vast overrepresentation. [3]

The primary researcher Bjornebekk said, "They are more vulnerable, they have experienced more trauma. Some of them come from violent cultures, and they take it along with them. Also, there are those who are not Oslo residents, who just come from other countries and only stay here for a few months."

They come from violent cultures, and they bring the violence along with them. The culture is, after all, an expression of the people that live in the land. A violent culture arises where there are violent people.

Another type of shock came when it was revealed that a former minister in Norway had gotten convicted for sexual bribery of three young asylum seeker males.

He demanded sex in return for an approval of their asylum request, threatening them with expulsion. All asylum seekers that came forward with these claims were men. [6]

Statistics Norway confirms a similar trend as witnessed in other countries. "The results show that both immigrants and Norwegian-born persons with two immigrant parents are overrepresented as registered offenders, with the rate of overrepresentation being highest in the latter group. Among immigrants, the overrepresentation is most substantial among family immigrants and refugees, as well as for individuals from African countries. For Asian immigrants the picture is more complex. Overall, Asian immigrants are overrepresented. However, while immigrants from certain Asian countries are similarly overrepresented, other Asian countries are underrepresented."

It can be expected that those from Afghanistan, Pakistan, and the Middle East are overrepresented, whereas those from China and Japan are underrepresented, as this would fit data from other sources. This expectation is matched by the data supplied later on in the research paper, where the Philippines, China, and India score relatively low, while Pakistan, Afghanistan, and so on, score relatively high.

"Individuals from Western Europe and North America, as well as education immigrants, are underrepresented as well." Once more the problem lies with the same groups of non-Western immigrants. "The pattern is, with some minor exceptions, relatively similar for Norwegian-born persons with two immigrant parents. The patterns of over- and underrepresentation also apply to most types of offenses... Overall the overrepresentation is substantially reduced when we account for differences in age and gender, especially in the groups with the highest rates of overrepresentation – including Norwegian-born persons with immigrant parents."

Substantially reduced is not the same as fully explained. Of course age and gender explains a portion, but the key message here is that it can't explain everything. Massive differences persist. "Place of residence and employment have limited explanatory power once the demographic differences are accounted for. For most immigrant groups a certain level overrepresentation persists also after sociodemographic characteristics are taken into account." Ultimately, overrepresentation continues for both first and second-generation immigrants from non-Western areas, most notably Africa, the Middle East, and South Asia. [4]

Sociodemographics is not quite the same as socioeconomics, it appears the researchers controlled for age and gender, but not for economic status.

Unfortunately major parts of the paper are written in Norwegian, making it somewhat less accessible to the public. The original authors and title are "Synøve N. Andersen, Bjart Holtsmark, Sigmund B. Mohn. Kriminalitet blant innvandrere og norskfødte med innvandrerforeldre. En analyse av registerdata for perioden 1992-2015." Translated to English, the title says "Crime among immigrants and Norwegian-born with immigrant parents. An analysis of register data for the period 1992-2015."

Their results, translated into English, tell us "Overall, the results reflect those we know from previous studies (see especially Skarðhamar, Thorsen and Henriksen, 2011). We find that there is a higher proportion perpetrators among both immigrants and Norwegian-born with immigrant parents compared to the rest of the population.

The proportion of perpetrators is highest among Norwegian-born with immigrant parents, which is a new discovery in the Norwegian context, but which have previously been found in other comparable countries, such as Sweden and Denmark (Andersen and Tranæs, 2011; Statistics Denmark, 2017; Kardell and Carlsson, 2009).

Differences in gender and age composition explain a good part of the overrepresentation, and age is a particularly important explanatory factor among Norwegian-born with immigrant parents. However, the over-representation consists of those most groups are initially overrepresented even after such factors is taken into account. Working immigrants are an important exception.

Furthermore, we find that it is significant variation in the proportion of perpetrators and accused persons after immigration background. Among immigrants, overrepresentation is particularly high among people with backgrounds from Asian and African countries, and among people who have received residence in Norway due to flight and family establishment or reunification. People with backgrounds from Western European and North American countries, as well educational immigrants, are underrepresented.

Also within each country group - and then especially in Asia - we find individual countries that are both overrepresented (including Turkey, Afghanistan, Iraq and Iran) and underrepresented (including the Philippines, India, China and Thailand). This illustrates once again what the group of immigrants is like heterogeneously composed and contributes in different ways and to varying degrees to the total the crime picture in Norway."

Rape

As mentioned, over 95% of street rapes in Oslo are at the hands of non-Western immigrants. The victims, on the other hand, are for the most part Norwegian women. In 2015 four asylum seekers from Syria raped their nineteen-year-old friend whom they knew before arriving in Norway. Since gang rapes are a fun activity that you'd like to remember, they recorded it. Please pardon my obvious sarcasm, but who would think it a good idea for any reason to record a gang rape on video? The footage is now used as evidence against them. [8]

One rape that made headlines and went viral was a Norwegian man that had been raped, but protested against his attacker getting deported. He believes the prison sentence was punishment enough. "Karsten Nordal Hauken, who describes himself as feminist and anti-racist, was sexually attacked five years ago. He said that although the incident caused a spiral of depression and substance abuse, he felt bad about the fact the man had been deported to Somalia when he had already served his prison sentence." Karsten then said, "But I also got a strong sense of guilt and responsibility. I was the reason why he should not be left in Norway, but rather to face a very uncertain future in Somalia." Well, Karsten, you are not the reason that he's getting expelled. The reason is that he raped you, and that it would be a shame if he were to rape in Norway again. There's a bit of prevention in the penalty. [9]

Eva Helgetun was fourteen years old when an immigrant violently raped her. During the rape, two other men entered the room. Eva believed this would be her rescue, but instead the immigrant men held her down while the first man raped her, and one of them tried to rape her afterwards as well. Luckily for Eva, she got away before that happened, and found safety in the arms of other Norwegians in the area. Still, Eva couldn't cope with what had happened, spiraled into depression, and ended up taking her own life. Suicide was the only way out for her. Her rapists were never caught, all we know is that they were non-Western in appearance. [10]

Education

The amount of rape by non-Western immigrants in Norway has led to a new concept in Norway, anti-rape classes. The classes are framed as simply being about how to treat women in Europe. It covers such topics such as women wearing a miniskirt, and whether that is normal or not. It is clarified to the immigrants that a woman dressed in a skirt is not an invitation for sex, and that she is not a prostitute.

Another discussion point highlights whether or not it is possible for a married man to rape his wife. The session includes a slide that asks the question 'What is sexual violence and rape?' But these are not children taking the course, they're adult men. Shouldn't we be able to expect from adult men, even coming from a different culture, that rape is wrong? If we need to teach them this, then isn't it fair to say that their culture is backwards and morally abhorrent? [7]

"He that makes himself a sheep shall be eaten by the wolf."

– Norwegian Saying

Notes:

[1] https://isgp-studies.com/immigration-the-rape-of-norway

[2] https://www.breitbart.com/europe/2020/02/23/migrants-vastly-overrepresented-in-norway-crime-stats/

[3] https://sputniknews.com/europe/201902281072829360-norway-violent-crime-immigrants/

[4] https://www.ssb.no/en/sosiale-forhold-og-kriminalitet/artikler-og-publikasjoner/_attachment/332143?_ts=16035d6f0d8

[5] https://summit.news/2019/09/06/integration-fail-new-study-in-norway-finds-children-of-migrants-commit-more-crime-than-their-parents/

[6] https://www.infomigrants.net/en/post/18051/former-norwegian-minister-sentenced-to-jail-for-sexually-abusing-asylum-seekers

[7]   https://www.bbc.com/news/world-europe-36469828

[8] https://www.rt.com/news/333269-migrants-rape-police-norway/

[9]
https://www.independent.co.uk/news/world/europe/
norwegian-rape-victim-feels-guilty-man-who-raped-
him-was-deported-a6975041.html

[10] https://gatesofvienna.net/2013/01/gang-rape-of-
a-child-in-trondheim/

EXPLORING EASTERN EUROPE

"Hungary will stop at nothing when it comes to protecting its citizens."

- Viktor Orban

What about crime in Eastern Europe?

A keen reader may have noticed that the countries we've discussed are those predominantly in western Europe. The Netherlands, Belgium, Germany, France, the United Kingdom, Ireland, Spain, Portugal, Italy, Greece, Norway, Sweden, and Finland. But what about Poland, the Czech Republic, Hungary, Lithuania, Latvia, Estonia, Iceland, Croatia, Slovakia, Slovenia, Serbia, Montenegro, Macedonia, Albania, Bosnia, Moldavia, Romania, Bulgaria, and even the Ukraine?

Poland, a country I've spent a little bit of time myself, does feel rather safe. Perhaps this experience is different in some small villages in the east, but police statistics appear to agree with my experience. "Polish National Police statistics underscore that Poland continues to be one of the safest countries in Europe." [1]

The Czech Republic sees mostly pickpocketing and petty theft. "Violent or confrontational crime is rare in the Czech Republic. Criminals rarely use violence or the threat of violence to perpetrate a crime, but since they could arm themselves with simple weapons such as knives, avoid direct confrontation." Overall safety in the Czech Republic is rated 'very high' during daylight and 'high' during nighttime. Most countries in Eastern Europe have similar scores. A country like France only scores 'moderate'. Even Ukraine scores slightly higher than France in this survey, despite being at poverty levels comparable to Africa and being in the middle of what must be called a civil war. Most notes on extreme violence in the Ukraine are linked to the warzone. I've visited cities in western Ukraine during the war, and the experience was very different. These cities were safe, and couldn't be compared to the excess violence taking place at the frontline. [2]

In Hungary crime is rather low as well. "Violent crime rates remain low in Hungary. There was a decrease in the number of homicides from 148 in 2018 to 141 in 2019. A large percentage of homicides are the result of domestic violence. Consequently, the successful investigation rate is high, since police are usually aware of the suspects." [3] When searching for articles on rape in Hungary, two articles appear on the front page. One is a Nigerian man that arrived as a student, who raped a prostitute. The other is a Somalian man that lured an intoxicated girl into a park, where he assaulted her, raped her, and stole her phone.

Despite all of these countries being poor compared to their western European counterparts, they have higher safety scores and there is less mention of violent crime. Despite them having rather few non-Western immigrants, the ones that are there already stand out in terms of crime.

Another lesson we can take from Eastern Europe comes in the form of their gypsy problem. Despite having arrived in Europe a thousand years ago, the gypsies are still overrepresented in a variety of crimes. [4] Once more this confirms that integration doesn't take place, and that living in a country for a few generations doesn't bring an end to issues that were present in the first generation. In the end, gypsies too form a group of non-Western immigrants, which is still identifiable even a millennium after their arrival.

Will the Turkish and Moroccans still be identifiable distinguished groups a thousand years later too? So far, there is nothing indicating they won't. Of course a section of the gypsies has merged into the general population as well, where intermarriage and interbreeding between gypsies and non-gypsies has taken place. Still, the gypsies remain in existence as a group, and locals tend to find it easy to tell who is a gypsy and who isn't. The biggest giveaway is the fact that gypsies have a darker skin.

The fact that these countries are so safe is curious for another reason, namely that they are all rather 'new'. Thirty years ago, the Soviet Union still acted as supreme overlord in these parts. In that sense, colonialism, often blamed for crime rates in the third world, has been gone longer than the Soviet Union. Still, whereas problems in Africa and the Middle East are still said to be a result from the colonial era, such excuses are less common when it comes to parts of Europe. Of course corruption in places like Romania is higher than in the Netherlands, and GDP per capita is lower, but overall the country is safe and things work.

I have visited most of the countries in this part of Europe. From the Balkans to the Baltics, from Prague to Kiev. These places feel comfortable, going to a bar is a pleasure, and the parks are filled with moms pushing around strollers. Compare it to walking around through Malmo, Rotterdam, London, Brussels, or Paris. The difference is clear.

"Saying you are a patriot is not enough - you have to be one."
- Janusz Korwin-Mikke

Notes:

[1]
https://www.osac.gov/Country/Poland/Content/Detail/Report/3534f2a5-7345-425f-b4a8-18cb84352741#:~:text=Polish%20National%20Police%20statistics%20underscore,U.S.%20nationals%20and%20other%20visitors.

[2]
https://www.osac.gov/Country/CzechRepublic/Content/Detail/Report/0d3db5a8-0af8-47ac-b035-18cb0e97cb75

[3]
https://www.osac.gov/Country/Hungary/Content/Detail/Report/5e577b60-b885-4c23-93dd-18cd8ec9758e#:~:text=Violent%20crime%20rates%20remain%20low,usually%20aware%20of%20the%20suspects.

[4]   https://www.bbc.com/news/world-europe-13544903

HELL AT HOME

In some of the other chapters, we've briefly reviewed crime statistics for places like the Dutch Caribbean and Pakistan, but we've so far ignored Africa and Afghanistan. It may be worth taking another look at these 'cultures of violence' that are plagued by war and civil strife.

What does it look like at home?

The immigrants that come from Africa and Islamic world to Europe, bring with them the same lifestyle that is prevalent in their home countries. Murder rates in Africa and South America are multiples of those in Europe. Where Europe has three murders per 100.000 inhabitants, Africa has more than twelve. That is four times as many, and ignores the fact that European murder rates include murders committed by non-Western immigrants. Lithuania has the highest rate among European countries, with still a relatively meagre 4.5 - far lower still than Africa. It is also worth noting that this data excludes victims from war, or those victims that simply go by unreported. [1]

"Official crime figures are not available for about half of all African countries, and those that do exist are rarely released on a regular basis. There are also problems with the reliability of police-recorded crime statistics, both in Africa and internationally. Many people do not report their victimization to the police, and those crimes that are reported are not always recorded by the authorities." [2]

As can be seen by the data on Numbeo, the data for many African countries is simply absent. These countries are also the most chaotic, and likely most criminal ones. Weak government and civil war creates an environment where crime can triumph. For the countries where data is available, or estimates can be made, crime rates are continuously higher than in Europe. China and Japan, on the other hand, are shown to have relatively low crime rates. This also matches the behavior of Chinese and Japanese immigrants in Europe, as they never show up overrepresented in European crime statistics. [3]

South Africa

South Africa is an example of a state that is approaching the level of a failed state. Crime and murder rates are increasing, and gang rapes are more and more common. [4] "A woman in South Africa is more likely to be raped than to learn to read, according to research from the One In Nine campaign. The police reported 68,332 sexual offences last year – an average of one every eight minutes – and one in four men surveyed by the Medical Research Council admitted committing rape. However, many of these crimes go unreported, with many victims remaining invisible, ignored not only by the media but by communities, police and courts." [7]

South Africa quite evidently has a rape culture. Rape has become normal, and happens frequently. How can such a rape epidemic be stopped? What are the causes? Or looked at from a different perspective... Won't inviting the inhabitants of such a place into Europe, bring with them the same rape culture? Is it effective to combat this issue by launching rape-prevention classes across Europe. Sure South Africa claims to counter the rape epidemic, but how reliable are its leaders?

"But the country's leaders have been accused of failing to practise what they preach. President Jacob Zuma, a traditional Zulu, has three wives and at least 21 children. He was cleared of rape in a trial, where he admitted sleeping with a family friend he knew to be HIV-positive. The Zulu king Goodwill Zwelithini, who has five wives, hosts an annual reed dance in which 25,000 bare-breasted women perform, after undergoing virginity tests." With such role models, is it any wonder the citizens act in such a way?

Rather than dropping onto one knee, and whipping out an expensive diamond, Africa has different ways of convincing a woman to marry a man. "As a largely patriarchal society, Africa has customs and traditions, since time immemorial, that have tolerated and promoted rape culture regardless of the community behind these cultures. One such ritual is the marriage ritual called Ukuthwala in the Nguni community in

South Africa. In this ritual, a young man of marriageable age would kidnap a girl or a young woman with the intention of compelling her family to approve the marriage and start negotiations." [13]

Sky News once published the details of interviews with South African rapists that explained why they did it. Since then, they have taken the page offline, leading to a 404 error. However, BuzzFeed wrote an article on the same topic, which is still online. In it, we can read a few of the interviews with South African rapists. What stands out is the complete lack of guilt. The men simply take what they want. In some cases, they offer the woman money in exchange for sex first, when the woman declines, they rape her. I will share some of the answers.

Person 1.
    "Q: How did it happen?
A: I always wanted the woman but because (I) am ugly and I knew that if I (tried) to (proposition) her she (would refuse) … unless I have a lot of money to buy her. I knew where she lived and traced her movements and how many people she lived with in her shack, but I found out that her boyfriend only came (back at) month ends. I went to her place Friday night and it was raining so it helped me attack her well as no one else could hear me. I used a bolt cutter to gain entry, wielding a butcher knife. I told her not to scream until I leave her place."

Person 2.
    "Q: How did it happen?

A: The woman always asked me for (a) cool drink or money for transport. I did give her (these things) many times. When I needed her to sleep with me she always came up with excuses. (In) January this year I met her on the street when I was coming from the nearby shop holding plastic (bags) with groceries. I decided to invite her to my place, she came over and when I needed sex she said, 'not today, next time'. I didn't buy the story. I overpowered and raped her."

Person 3.
"Q: How did it happen?
A: We watched (a) game of soccer together at my place at night while her parents had gone out. I bought some ciders. I knew she liked them, and we drunk together. In the middle of the game I (raped her).

Q: Did she open a case against you?
A: No!

Q: Why not?
A: I think she just got scared of her parents and avoided the embarrassment.

Q: Have you apologised to her to see if she had animosity towards you after the rape?
A: I tried but she didn't want to talk to me.

Q: How do you feel that you did such a thing to your neighbour?
A: I feel great because she is a nice woman to have (slept) with even though (it was) against her will."

Rather than guilt, the man feels a certain pride for having had sex with an attractive woman.

Person 4.

"Q: How did it happen?

A: My ex-girlfriend's sister lived with us in the same shack and when (I was) off her sister would be at work, so we watched TV together. I asked and promised to buy her expensive shoes if she slept with me. She refused and I forced myself on her and told her that if she talked about it I would chase both her (and) her sister, so she kept quiet.

Q: How do you feel whenever you see her after you did this?

A: I feel nothing bad about it.

Q: Why not?

A: I supported her at my place and I deserved to ask for a favour too.

Q: Do you call it rape?

A: No.

Q: But you forced yourself on her?

A: Yes."

Apparently non-consensual sex accompanied by threaths of violence do not constitute rape in this man's mind.

Person 5.

"Q: How did it happen?

A: Fridays we went out to chill and drink some beers ... after hours me and my friend we saw a young good-looking woman who was drunk on the street, we took her to our place and (raped) her in our shack for an hour. This became a habit and every Friday we made sure that we hung on at the tavern to pick up girls who were drinking after hours.

Q: How many times have you raped a woman?
A: Five times.

Q: Have you ever been arrested for any rape?
A: Once.

Q: Did you serve time for it?
A: Yes.

Q: How long?
A: Six years.

Q: Do you think it's the right thing to do?
A: Why do women go to taverns in mini-skirts?

Q: What do you think they want?
A: To be raped."

Most of these men didn't even go to jail for their crimes. Either they weren't caught, or there wasn't enough evidence against them. They all feel rather justified in their actions, and feel no guilt or remorse, there is no empathy towards the victim. Not all men in South Africa are likely to think like this, but with the high rape-rates in the country, there is a significant portion of men that do act and think like this. Moreover, it is likely not restricted to South Africa, but prevalent across the continent. With such attitudes toward rape, we shouldn't be surprised to see an increase in rapes in Europe as well. [14]

Afghanistan

A similar situation is present in Afghanistan. Tribal leaders abuse their position to gang rape girls as they please. [8] A kidnapped family saw the mother raped by multiple Taliban men after dragging her husband from the cell. After the ordeal was over, she was left lying naked on the ground. It isn't clear whether the children had to watch, or if they were kept elsewhere. [9]

Such rapes aren't too exceptional in Afghanistan. "Afghan police have arrested six men in connection with the brutal gang rape of four women last month in Kabul, the Wall Street Journal reported. The attack, which included an 18-year-old and a pregnant woman among the victims, has shocked many in an increasingly lawless Afghanistan, where rapes are rarely prosecuted or even reported. Afghan police announced the arrests on Tuesday. That same day one of the four victims died in a hospital, public health officials told Khaama Press, an Afghan news site." [10]

The attackers pretended to be Afghan police, halting the car the victims were in for a supposedly random checkpoint. Once the cars stopped, the women were dragged from the cars and raped in front of their families. Afghan judges, however, did not show leniency comparable to that given by European judges. The men were hanged. [11]

The United States military has a kind of 'don't ask, don't tell' policy towards sexual abuse in Afghanistan. Although the US soldiers are of course not allowed to go around and rape Afghan women, they are to look the other way when they witness rape as it is deemed to be a cultural issue. The 'dancing boys' are allowed to exist, despite it being nothing but young boys getting raped by old men.

The training given to the American soldiers states, "Although sexual assault is against the law in almost all countries, the laws are not always enforced to protect the victims. In fact, in some countries, shame and stigma are often attached to the victim and not the offender. Victims also risk blame and punishment for the crime that was committed against them."

A rape victim isn't celebrated as a survivor, but faces shame and judgement. One practice the Afghani use is that the victim needs to marry the rapist, who thereby goes unpunished for his crime, while the victim has to spend the rest of her life with her attacker.

Similar practices are witnessed in areas of Africa. Is this the type of cultural enrichment we want in Europe though? Because hypothetically, if we would replace 50% of the European populace by people from such cultures, wouldn't the European culture change and become exactly like the ones we see here? [12]

Global rankings

Another metric to look at is that of the world's safest countries. Different websites give slightly different rankings, but the variance is limited. Countries that show up in the top are places like Norway, Iceland, Switzerland, Portugal, Finland, and other European countries, as well as Japan, New Zealand, Canada, Singapore, Qatar and Dubai. African and South American countries don't appear on the lists. World Population Review gives us the following top ten: Iceland, New Zealand, Portugal, Austria, Denmark, Canada, Singapore, Czech Republic, Japan, and Switzerland. [6]

Countries that are considered the most dangerous, with a severe travel risk are: Afghanistan, Central African Republic, Iraq, Libya, Mali, Somalia, South Sudan, Syria, and Yemen. [5] Fair is fair, some of those on the list are there due to Western military intervention. This is not something I personally promote or condone. Especially for a country like Libya it is worth noting that until it was sent into civil war and complete anarchy at the hands of Western militaries, it scored a lot better with regards to safety. However, not all countries on the list have that same excuse.

All reasons given to justify higher crime statistics for these immigrants from places like Afghanistan and Africa just don't add up when we take into account that the same problems exist in their home countries. To claim that it's due to racism, prejudice, and so on, it doesn't make sense. Poverty may explain why there is more theft in such places, but the type of violence and groups of men raping women and feeling no remorse, that is not explained by a lower GDP per capita. In essence, what we witness is that criminal behavior for these groups in Europe is very similar to their criminal behavior in their home countries. That means that if we're importing these people and their culture, we're also importing their crime statistics.

Yet these are countries that have negative travel advice given by European governments, precisely due to their crime rates. So far, we can avoid the problem by avoiding visits to those countries. We can avoid the problem by avoiding certain cities and neighborhoods in Europe. By not going onto the street late at night, by having someone escort girls to their homes.

But what when the problem keeps growing? Will we voluntarily reduce our freedom of movement in order to obtain our safety? The same level of safety that we've had before mass immigration of non-Western groups, at a point in time where we still had freedom of movement. Will we surrender our freedoms to remain safe?

"They who can give up essential liberty to obtain a little temporary safety deserve neither liberty nor safety."

— Benjamin Franklin

Notes:

[1] https://dataunodc.un.org/crime/intentional-homicide-victims

[2] https://www.unodc.org/documents/data-and-analysis/Africa_%20Report_full_2005.pdf

[3] https://www.numbeo.com/crime/rankings_by_country.jsp?title=2020

[4] https://www.bbc.com/news/world-africa-48093708

[5] https://www.atlasandboots.com/travel-blog/most-dangerous-countries-in-the-world/

[6] https://worldpopulationreview.com/country-rankings/safest-countries-in-the-world

[7] https://www.theguardian.com/lifeandstyle/2010/nov/18/south-africa-murder-rape

[8] https://www.youtube.com/watch?v=WjiijjN_uV8

[9] https://www.independent.co.uk/news/world/middle-east/taliban-hostages-caitlan-coleman-boyle-joshua-gang-rape-assault-experiences-family-children-afghanistan-a8066991.html

[10] https://www.buzzfeednews.com/article/miriamberger/outrage-grows-over-brutal-gang-rape-in-afghanistan

[11] https://www.independent.co.uk/news/world/middle-east/five-men-executed-afghanistan-gang-rape-9782443.html

[12] https://www.thedailybeast.com/marines-trained-that-rape-in-afghanistan-is-a-cultural-issue

[13] https://face2faceafrica.com/article/history-of-rape-culture-and-how-african-customs-promote-it

[14] https://www.buzzfeednews.com/article/alisonvingiano/a-group-of-south-african-men-explained-why-they-raped

Epilogue

"The thought police would get him just the same. He had committed--would have committed, even if he had never set pen to paper--the essential crime that contained all others in itself. Thoughtcrime, they called it. Thoughtcrime was not a thing that could be concealed forever. You might dodge successfully for a while, even for years, but sooner or later they were bound to get you."
-   George Orwell

There is plenty of research that indicates immigrants are less criminal than other citizens. Nearly all of this research, however, stems from the United States, and is highly influenced by the high degree of crime committed by African Americans. In Europe, it is known and admitted by all serious investigators that immigrants are overrepresented in crime statistics.

Science is on the side of those that admit migrant crime in Europe is a serious issue that needs to be openly discussed and addressed. It is counterproductive to claim all such criticisms are founded in pure racism, or that discussing it would play into the hands of the far-right political parties. Even if it plays into the hands of the far-right political parties, is it thereby wrong? Is that a good reason not to discuss it? We do not say climate science 'plays into the hands' of the left-wing political parties. No, science is impartial. Though, sticking to our 1984 reference, we can add in the quote "In Newspeak there is no word for 'Science.'"

One scientific paper that we've consulted is a document written by Martin Killias, titled 'Immigration and Crime: The European Experience'. The document was written in 2011 and has received funding from the European Union itself. Martin Killias is linked to the University of Zurich, he's an expert in criminology and has received multiple prestigious awards for his work. It should give his words some credibility. "The paper concludes that crime among migrants is a problem that policy-makers should not ignore." [1]

The paper states, "It has become usual to depict migration as being completely independent of negative side-effects such as higher crime rates. The research that has been reviewed in this paper does not warrant such a conclusion, however. Not at all periods (i.e. not before 1970) and not everywhere (not in the USA), but in most European countries of the present period, crime is more prevalent among minorities. The higher offending rates among migrants according to court and police statistics cannot be explained away by disproportionate risks of being reported to the police, to be known to the police as an offender, to be prosecuted or convicted – and finally sentenced to custody." It goes on, "Accepting the empirical fact offending rates are higher among migrants is not a way of blackmailing them even further. Rather, it is the precondition to develop strategies of prevention that may greatly improve the quality of life both for the majority and the minorities."

Youth

One of the arguments against migrants causing more crime is that, even though they do cause more crime, this can be explained by the fact that migrants are mostly young men. Young men, in any society, are the ones that commit most crimes. It is true that this explains a portion of the violence, but every country that provides us with statistics where age is included as a factor shows us that even in the same age categories the immigrants show more criminal behavior. The portion explained by age is, in the end, relatively small.

Moreover, in the section on Norway we discussed a study that corrected for such demographic elements. On top of that, we've seen in the Dutch and British data that overrepresentation persisted, even when filtering for age categories.

The Media

Another piece of flawed logic says that we only perceive immigrants to be more criminal, because the media jumps on high-profile immigrant crime and the news goes viral. This would imply that such articles are cherry-picked, and do not reflect reality.

That, unfortunately, is easily debunked when we look at the statistics. Every country that has statistics shows us that all together immigrants are indeed more criminal. The anecdotal evidence matches completely with the statistical evidence. Immigrants, especially from non-Western countries, are overrepresented in the amount of suspects, arrests, convictions, and prison populations.

Prejudice

Those that acknowledge that immigrants are overrepresented in the statistics, try to attack the validity of these statistics. They claim that the reason more criminals end up in jail, is due to institutional prejudice and racism on behalf of the police, the judges, and the entirety of our legal system. However, if the police were racist, while judges were not, we should see an increase in the amount of immigrant suspects and arrests, but relatively few convictions as the judges can correct the faulty police work. We do not see this trend.

If the judges were racist, while police were not, we should see that relatively few immigrant suspects and arrests result in a relatively high degree of convictions. We do not see this trend.

Lastly, we could hypothesize that judges and police are equally racist. However, since we see this trend across Europe, it would mean that such racism is prevalent across Europe to very similar degrees. A judge in Italy would have to be as racist as a Swedish police officer. It is rather unlikely. In fact, we see the opposite is true. Judges are often rather progressive and liberal, and actively avoid any opportunity for their opponents to label them as racist.

We have seen many examples of cases where violent crime is penalized with ridiculously low penalties. Where foreign culture and misunderstanding the local laws has been used to justify these mild convictions. Convictions that are in some cases perhaps even milder than a native person would receive.

Let's not forget the grooming gang in Rotherham, which was ignored by the government for not wanting to appear racist in tackling a Pakistani gang. It appears that racist beliefs in the judicial system are non-existent, and a pure figment of imagination of those that wish to believe that immigrants are not more criminal, that there is an alternative reason. The hypothesis simply holds no ground.

Even if the police applies racial profiling, it is somewhat justifiable when we look at the vast overrepresentation of some groups. If we know that a Moroccan is five times more likely to engage in criminal behavior, it means that a dodgy looking Moroccan gives us a high likelihood of actually being a criminal.

Moreover, racial profiling does not frame people that are innocent. It only catches actual criminals. If people don't commit crimes, racial profiling is nothing but a mild nuisance. Such racial profiling may be more likely to turn up those in possession of illegal drugs or firearms, but it won't influence the rate of convictions for rape, theft, and murder. It is not racial profiling that plants DNA evidence (semen) on the victim of a gang rape. The arrests for immigrants for such 'low impact' crimes such as drug possession, don't stand out in comparison to the arrests made for rape, violent crime, or theft. So it seems that even if racial profiling takes place, which begs the question to begin with since most police forces are very politically correct, it doesn't have any serious impact on crime statistics.

In any case, institutional racism is a bogus claim for which evidence is lacking. On top of the lacking evidence, it is simply absurd to claim that equal degrees of institutional racism are present in all layers of the judicial system in all parts of Europe.

Even a piece of general pro-immigration research from Greece is forced to conclude that "There is hard evidence that immigration has increased criminality to a very substantial extent in the categories of serious crimes. The crime rates of immigrants are much higher than those of Greeks for all years for which there are available data... There is much talk about evident racism and xenophobia in Greece with all its negative consequences for both immigrants and Greeks. However, there is no evidence, apart from isolated incidents, to support the view that the Greek society as an organized whole with its institutions and laws shows signs of racism and xenophobia." [2]

Lastly, on the topic of prejudice and racism, it is somewhat odd that it would only apply to those from the Islamic world and Africa. Wouldn't the same prejudice apply to the Chinese? To the Indians? People from India and Pakistan are rather similar in appearance, though Pakistani men are significantly more criminal than those from India. If the root cause of it all was prejudice, wouldn't the ignorant police officers treat both of these groups in the same way? Appearance is similar, though culture is different. The effect shows in the results.

Wouldn't racists hate the Chinese as much as the Africans? Such claims of racism and prejudice are uttered by those that acknowledge crime data being skewed in a clear direction, but that refuse to put any blame on the criminal groups. In an attempt to dismantle the far-right political parties, they take blame away from the criminal immigrants, and instead place blame on the racist beliefs of the far-right politicians and their supporters.

Illegality

Some try to claim that it makes perfect sense that immigrants commit more crimes, because they have no other choice. Those that are in the country illegally cannot find a normal job, and are reduced to theft and prostitution. That is true, but that would only apply to those that are actually illegally in the country.

Crime statistics, however, show that also legal immigrants and even second-generation immigrants are overrepresented in crime statistics. That alone reduces this argument to dust.

Economics

There is indeed a correlation between socio-economic status and crime. To simplify this statement; poor people commit more crime. Now the logic would go that since non-Western immigrants tend to be relatively poor due to a lack of proper education and difficulties with the new language and customs, that this low socio-economic status drives them towards criminal behavior. This is not a very strong statement, though proper research is unfortunately lacking.

Even the countries that track crime statistics don't offer the ability to sort by income. It is likely that this explains a portion of the increased crime rates. However, this is likely a very small portion. Western Europe has seen millions of immigrants come from Poland, Romania, Bulgaria, the Ukraine, and so on. It has received refugees from Yugoslavia when the country broke up into nation-states. All of these groups arrived as poor workers with a poor understanding of the local language, doing simple lowly paid jobs. And data does show that these groups are a bit more criminal, primarily when it comes to theft. The stereotypical types of crime are Romanian pickpockets and stolen cars that end up in Poland. They score a bit higher on other types of crime as well, but differences are relatively minor. This is what we would expect from groups that are lower on the socio-economic ladder.

Non-Western immigrants, on the other hand, show vastly higher increases of crime across all categories. Being poor may be a justification for theft, such as Jean Valjean in *Les Miserables* who claims he merely stole a loaf of bread, for his sister's child was close to death. Yet, it forms a poorer justification for violent gang rape, or rape in general. It forms a poor explanation for terrorism, and it forms a poor explanation for grooming gangs. It forms a poor explanation for murder, for excess violence, for aggression, and so on. So not only do proponents of this logic hold that poverty turns us into remorseless monsters, it also fails to explain why poor immigrants from Eastern Europe show very different criminal behaviors compared to non-Western immigrants. Overall, the theory is bunk.

The Real Reasons

So what is left? What are the reasons that non-Western immigrants are so overrepresented in crime statistics?

Number one is culture. Especially Islamic culture. Not only is the position of women in Islam notably lower than that of men, but more important is the position of non-believing women. Infidel women. There is no coincidence in the fact that grooming gangs, rape gangs, and overall rapes committed by Muslim men target non-Muslim women. The men fail to show remorse for their crimes, and speak about the women they rape as trash, as white bitches, white whores, and so on. In some cases, we saw that they decided to actively allow Muslim girls that they accidentally abducted to leave without harm done, while they attacked the non-Muslim girl. This is clear evidence of it not being violence towards women in general, but violence towards non-Muslim women. Clearly, in the minds of these Muslim men, such women are worthless. This is confirmed by many women walking the streets, getting catcalled and hearing the word 'whore' ring in their ear when they walk through Muslim neighborhoods.

Number two is a painful topic. When we talk about African men, we have to acknowledge that they show up globally as having increased crime rates. This applies to the United States, to the United Kingdom, to the Netherlands, and even to Africa itself. Can it be explained due to socio-economic status? Evidence differs, but this is unlikely for the same reason as we discussed previously when talking about non-Western immigrants in general. [3]

Is it cultural? A portion of African immigrants also adheres to the Muslim faith, which can explain some behaviors, but a large portion of Africans are Christians. Of course, religion is not the entirety of one's culture. But are there other overarching elements of African culture that persist globally in black populations? Can culture explain why African-American blacks are equally criminal and violent as those that live in the United Kingdom? Are those that come straight from Nigeria equal in culture to those that arrive from Jamaica? This just doesn't seem entirely convincing. There are cultural similarities between blacks living in the United States and the United Kingdom, but how culturally similar are those from Somalia and Jamaica? All are overrepresented in crime data.

An overarching culture could exist in the American export of black gangster and hip hop culture. This could be a subculture that appeals to a large subset of Africans that are living in Europe. So, it is possible that the gangster culture promoted by the American music industry creates a culture of violence and crime. On the other hand, is it a likely scenario that those with African ancestry are appealed by the same type of music globally and change their behavior based on that? Other groups listen to gangster rap as well, without it changing their behavior. Or, is gangster rap simply an expression, coming as a result from the crime-filled lifestyle of American blacks? So, it becomes a chicken and egg story. What came first, gangster culture, or gangster behavior? Or, do they reinforce one another?

One aspect that applies to all of them is, quite frankly, that they look different from the natives of Europe. Melanin in the skin changes the skin tone, as much as we wish to state all people are exactly the same, visual differences persist. Skin tone differences could lead to a feeling of not belonging, the feeling of being an outsider. Thereby, even when racism and discrimination are absent, these groups distance themselves from society, believing they don't fit in anyway. That could push people, in theory, into a life of crime.

This, nevertheless, doesn't explain why crime rates are higher in their home countries as well. It doesn't explain why crime rates in nearly exclusive black cities or neighborhoods in for example the United States aren't lower as you would expect following that hypothesis.

It begs the question if there is a wide variety of different reasons, of which at least one applies to groups of blacks all around the globe, or if there is one overarching reason that drives criminal behavior. The multiple reason hypothesis works by stating that crime in Africa is higher due to corruption and poverty. Crime by blacks in the United States is higher due to a history of slavery. Crime by blacks in Europe is higher due to perceived racism, or due to a lower socio-economic status. The single overarching reason hypothesis would imply that there is an underlying factor that affects blacks globally.

An example would be the highly controversial IQ. Both Africans, as well as blacks in the United States and Europe, score lower than average on IQ tests. Although the validity of these tests is highly debated, as some claim the tests are insensitive to cultural differences and thereby rendered useless, it is a fact that blacks do score lower on these tests. If we were to assume their validity is in order, then we could wonder if there could be a connection between IQ and crime. That would indicate that the overall lower IQ of black people brings about a higher than average tendency towards criminal behavior.

Such a genetic root cause is extremely controversial, and difficult to prove either way. It tends to be a point beyond the realm of discussion, as any attempt to do so will simply see one group labelled as racists, Nazi's, or both. Raising the question puts one on the same moral level as literally Adolf Hitler, according to most of the politically correct world. Now, despite this book being rather politically incorrect and 'on the edge' of permissible debate, I am reluctant to cross that line. I'm reluctant to conclude that there is a deterministic factor that causes black crime rates to be above average. At the same time, I'm not sure what the other reason could be. Once we acknowledge that the group does commit more crime, more research can be done to find out what the root cause may be.

As mentioned before; youth, prejudice, or the media can't seem to explain the behaviors either. Is it the fact that more black men are raised by single mothers? If that were the case, then our modern world is looking at an upcoming crime wave as more and more nuclear families have fallen apart. Yet evidence for this point appears to be absent, and the claim is based on the fact that American blacks are often raised in fatherless homes, while at the same time they engage in more criminal behavior. However, is this a correlation or a causal relationship? Or, is there something that explains both the increase in criminal behavior, as well as the fatherless homes? An underlying root cause that would explain black crime rates, as well as fatherless homes.

At this point, very little remains that can be said without a book getting banned. Nobody bats an eye when I say that the Japanese are generally, as a people, less violent than European whites. Their lower testosterone and their superb control of their emotions keeps them out of trouble, something witnessed by the crime data from Japan. However, this statement would also mean that the Japanese, as a people, are less violent than Africans. Suddenly, the statement is racist.

Though, is it racist to state that blacks have higher testosterone levels than whites? The statement is true, blacks have testosterone levels around 20% higher than whites. [4] Testosterone could be a connection to crime. And indeed, evidence suggests that higher testosterone is linked to more violent crime. [5]

This explanation would also clarify why crime rates have been dropping in the developed world, because simultaneously testosterone levels have been dropping as well. As a secondary observation, it explains the differences in violent crime between men and women. Obesity and a sedentary lifestyle, a life where conflict is replaced with comfort, and struggle with satisfaction - it all lowers testosterone.

If blacks are less affected by these downsides of modern life, and their testosterone levels remain higher, or alternatively, were higher initially, and have a longer way to drop, that could do a very good job at explaining the differences in criminal behavior. The question then remains, what can we do about it? It is difficult to see who has high testosterone and who does not. Should we discriminate against those with high testosterone levels? Should we take precautions and send those with higher levels to rape-prevention classes? Should we only grant asylum to those with lower testosterone levels? Should we, and here it becomes really sketchy, actively target those with elevated levels and take action to lower them?

Now, I must admit here as well that the connection between testosterone and criminal behavior is not perfect. Can a 20% increase in average testosterone levels explain a crime rate that's the quadruple? Frankly, I don't know. It is a topic worth investigating, but I will leave it to someone else.

Another possibility for the increase in all forms of crime is a general distance from the individual to society as a whole. Non-Western immigrants see these progressive liberal societies, and they simply don't feel like they are a part of it. They see the Europeans as strangers, for which they lack a sense of solidarity. This may be a huge and ignored issue, caused by the absence of integration. Let's not forget that integration without assimilation is a myth, a nonsensical term used to apply wishful thinking and dream about a functioning multicultural society. In essence, a multicultural society does not imply integration takes place at all, it implies that multiple cultures live in the same geographical area. But what if some of those cultures don't feel this feeling of solidarity to the other cultures? Suddenly, it becomes okay to steal from them.

It becomes okay to fake illness and to pull in government subsidies. It becomes okay to avoid taxes, to deal drugs, and so on.

Some may at this point wish to hear a solution to this very real problem. My proposed solution is simple. Put an end to non-Western immigration immediately. A government has a mandate to govern the people, on grounds of an implicit promise to protect the people of that nation. Right now, government policies of open borders are endangering the people inhabiting the European countries, pumping up their crime rates and creating an unsafe environment. Already women are afraid to go out at night on their own in certain areas. The government is failing its duty, it's failing to provide adequate protection to its citizens, and to act in their best interest. Only those that believe the world is one big happy family, may consider it acceptable to surrender their own safety.

Closing the borders is a big move, and will see a lot of opposition. Yet, there is a critical problem with keeping the borders open. We know for a fact, after reading this book, that at the moment immigrants from non-Western regions bring crime to our villages, towns, and cities. We are not sure what the reason for it is, which is one problem.

Though, even if we were 100% sure what caused it, the question remains - can we solve it? If the problem is socioeconomics, can we actually reduce it? If the problem is a movement of self-distancing, can we remove that? If the problem lies with the culture and the Islamic faith, can we convert people? If the problem sits with testosterone levels, can we reduce them?

Unless we have a solution ready, of which we know it'll work, we are sacrificing the lives of our own citizens for the sake of a multicultural dream of harmony. And there the question becomes, is that justifiable? Perhaps a better question; are the lives of the Danish natives that the Danish government has a mandate to protect worth more than the lives of Somalian refugees?

And for those fleeing safe areas of the world, are their improved economic prospects and quality of life worth more than the girl that has to live her life with a traumatic rape experience? Is that worth more than the person that gets killed in an act of random violence? Here it becomes a moral dilemma. The existence of this moral dilemma, however, is denied.

Politicians don't tell us that the girls that get raped are a worthy trade-off to make the multicultural society a reality. They don't tell us that the ones that get stabbed to death, do so in order for foreigners to work here and pay for the pensions of the elderly. (A myth that I've debunked in my previous book, 'The Migration Myth'.)

If voters are presented with the choice to sacrifice their safety for the wellbeing of the immigrants, are they going to be willing to vote for such open border policies? Will they wash their hands in innocence? Or will the fear of blood sticking to their own hands push them to vote for a different direction?

Right now, voters are not allowed to make a rational decision, as the crime data for most countries is not even published. Countries actively try to hide reality, as they fear it could support people voting for right wing parties. What does that tell us about the government apparatus? Does it not show that they have a clear goal in mind, and that the will of the voter is a mere nuisance? Should not the goal be to have an informed populace that can make and is allowed to make their own decisions? Isn't transparency a key value for a functioning democracy?

Then, dear governments, start publishing this data. Dear media, start reporting on the clear-as-day differences. Dear politicians, stop using nonsense excuses to deny the validity of the data. Dear voters, acknowledge that we have a problem that exists Europe-wide. A problem affecting our safety, as well as the safety of our children. A problem that will not go away with a few generations, but a problem that persists, and a problem that grows as our borders remain open.

Non-Western immigrants bring the poverty, war, and violence that they grew up in with them. And their children continue to carry it onwards. The places they come from weren't violent due to the characteristics of the environment, they were violent due to the presence of the people that lived there. Integration, as shown by data on second-generation immigrants, is a myth and will not happen.

Hence, governments need to punish criminals harder, and reinstate banishment as a penalty. Send people back to their home countries when they are first-generation immigrants when they commit any type of serious crime. Send them back and never allow them to return to Europe. Commit to building border fences and patrols in order to secure the borders. This is fairly simply as only southern Spain and the border with Turkey would need fencing, while navy patrols can guard the Mediterranean.

For the immigrants already in Europe, offer remigration funds. For those that wish to stay, place efforts into instilling European culture onto them. Closely control Islam, and consider banning the religion completely. The adherents of Islam have shown too much disregard for European women, and too many mosques have invited radical Islamic preachers that come and sow discontent.

In order to remove the most violent elements from society, bring back the life sentence. Retribution and safety is more important than their bright reintegration outcome. Reintegration is not a feasible outcome for those that were not integrated to begin with. Not all immigrants are criminals, nobody has stated that. Yet a high enough portion are for it to be a societal problem. The criminal elements need to be eliminated to protect the safe and high-trust societies that Europe has built over the last centuries.

The Victims

I believe it is the right thing to do, to end with a reference to the victims. Behind all these statistics hide real people, with real trauma, real loss, and real suffering. It is for that reason that I've included many pieces of anecdotal evidence. I hope these anecdotes clarify the extent of the horror that these people have gone through. The anecdotes included in this book are only a small sample. In reality, the suffering is greater than any of us can comprehend.

Moreover, statistics are numbers that cannot explain properly the differences between crimes. Your phone getting stolen is annoying, but not traumatic. Getting violently raped by a group of strangers is different.

There is one more critical difference that makes this type of violence so scary. Generally, crime has been either theft, looking for easy targets, while the more violent crime was restricted to those active in for example the drug trade. Criminals would shoot criminals. With regards to rape, it was mostly done by people you knew. Although getting raped by a friend isn't much better than getting raped by a stranger, as it also damages your interpersonal trust, there is a feeling of control. You control who you meet and who you hang out with. You control whether you become active in the underworld or not.

Yet non-Western immigrants seem to target anyone. It becomes seemingly random. It could happen to anyone, regardless of how many precautions you take. Another crucial difference is how they are active mostly in groups. Whereas 'regular' criminals such as rapists tend to act alone, now there are entire networks that cooperate, and bond over it.

The tragic part is that all of the suffering discussed in this book could have been prevented. It could have been prevented by having stricter rules for immigration, rather than allowing everybody that wants to into the country.

Europe could be a safe place, where you don't need to worry when going out onto the street late at night. A place where you are not afraid when your child is out of your vision at the playground for a minute. A place where you are not anxious when your daughter leaves the house alone. A safe and pleasant place. A utopia.

We can continue to deny the impact that non-Western immigrants have on crime. Like an ostrich, we too can stick our heads in the sand, or walk around with a blindfold. We can pretend not to see the reality around us, but what will we achieve by doing so? Slowly, bit by bit, our countries will degrade into the likes of South-Africa. Gated communities will rise up, as people become willing to pay a premium in order to remain safe.

When you have reached this part, I would ask you to lay down the book next to you, and take a minute of silence. A minute to think about the victims of these unnecessary crimes. A moment to acknowledge their suffering. And ask yourself. For what? What did we accomplish with our open border policies? Was it worth it?

"Man grows used to everything, the scoundrel!"

— *Fyodor Dostoevsky*

Notes:

[1]
https://cadmus.eui.eu/bitstream/handle/1814/1896
0/EU-
US%20Immigration%20Systems%202011_19.pdf?sequ
ence=1&isAllowed=y

[2]   https://ec.europa.eu/home-
affairs/sites/homeaffairs/files/what-we-
do/networks/european_migration_network/reports/do
cs/emn-studies/illegally-resident/gr-finalstudy_en.pdf

[3]
https://www.channel4.com/news/factcheck/factchec
k-black-americans-commit-crime

[4] https://pubmed.ncbi.nlm.nih.gov/3455741/

[5]
https://www.ncbi.nlm.nih.gov/pmc/articles/PMC369
3622/#:~:text=effects%20their%20realization.-
,There%20is%20evidence%20that%20testosterone%20
levels%20are%20higher%20in%20individuals,aggressi
ve%20phases%20of%20sports%20games.

ABOUT THE AUTHOR

Joseph R. Oxfield is the author of 'The Migration Myth' and has now published his second book. The founder of the Clovis Institute has written previously for websites like the Voice of Europe and The Old Continent, among others. He has lived in three countries in Europe, and has visited nearly all the others at least once. He has witnessed the increases in crime during his time in Luton and his visits to Paris. In the end, he wanted to research what the influence of immigrants on the feeling of insecurity was. The result is what you have just read.

You can reach him on jroxfield@gmail.com, or visit www.clovisinsitute.org to read more articles. Don't hesitate to reach out.